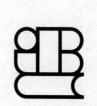

**University
of Michigan
Business
School** Management Series

INNOVATIVE SOLUTIONS TO THE
PRESSING PROBLEMS OF BUSINESS

The mission of the University of Michigan Business School Management Series is to provide accessible, practical, and cutting-edge solutions to the most critical challenges facing businesspeople today. The UMBS Management Series provides concepts and tools for people who seek to make a significant difference in their organizations. Drawing on the research and experience of faculty at the University of Michigan Business School, the books are written to stretch thinking while providing practical, focused, and innovative solutions to the pressing problems of business.

Executive Summary

This book tells how to create an integrated customer measurement and management system that will help your company allocate resources and increase profits. Whether you are an executive enabling others through training and support or a specialist within a department that collects, analyzes, or uses customer data to improve quality, satisfaction, and customer loyalty, the book provides the tools and skills that you will need to tailor a customer measurement and management system to your company.

The book describes five stages in developing the system.

- **Stage 1** (Chapter Two): Identify the system's purpose and goals, deciding which customers to include and how to group them into natural segments that reflect their interests and purchasing patterns.
- **Stage 2** (Chapter Three): Use qualitative research to build the "lens of the customer," a model of customer views of the products and services that you provide, customer satisfaction, and the loyalty and retention that result.

- **Stage 3** (Chapter Four): Use the lens of the customer to build a customer survey to measure quality, satisfaction, and loyalty.
- **Stage 4** (Chapter Five): Use the lens again in analyzing data from the customer survey, both to determine what could be done to improve customer satisfaction and to assess the probable effect of each potential improvement on bottom-line financial performance.
- **Stage 5** (Chapter Six): Set priorities for quality improvement, using the information developed from the survey as background for business decisions, and then implement the decisions according to the priorities set by management.

Within each stage, we provide step-by-step processes for developing an integrated customer measurement and management system. Creating a system that links quality, satisfaction, loyalty, and profit closes the loop. The key is to view quality, satisfaction, or loyalty not as separate concepts or passing fads that can be substituted for one another but rather as aspects of an overall system that enhances the bottom line.

Improving Customer Satisfaction, Loyalty, and Profit

An Integrated Measurement and Management System

Michael D. Johnson

Anders Gustafsson

JOSSEY-BASS
A Wiley Company
San Francisco

Library of Congress Cataloging-in-Publication Data

Johnson, Michael D. (Michael David)
    Improving customer satisfaction, loyalty, and profit : an integrated measurement and management system / Michael D. Johnson, Anders Gustafsson.— 1st ed.
        p. cm. — (The University of Michigan Business School management series)
    Includes bibliographical references and index.
    ISBN 0-7879-5310-5
    1. Consumer satisfaction. 2. Customer loyalty. 3. Customer relations. I. Gustafsson, Anders, date. II. Title. III. Series.
    HF5415.335 .J64 2000
    658.8'12—dc21   00-009245

FIRST EDITION
HB Printing   10 9 8 7 6 5 4 3 2 1

Contents

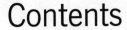

Foreword

Welcome to the University of Michigan Business School Management Series. The books in this series address the most urgent problems facing business today. The series is part of a larger initiative at the University of Michigan Business School (UMBS) that ties together a range of efforts to create and share knowledge through conferences, survey research, interactive and distance training, print publications, and new media.

It is just this type of broad-based initiative that sparked my love affair with UMBS in 1984. From the day I arrived I was enamored with the quality of the research, the quality of the MBA program, and the quality of the Executive Education Center. Here was a business school committed to new lines of research, new ways of teaching, and the practical application of ideas. It was a place where innovative thinking could result in tangible outcomes.

The UMBS Management Series is one very important outcome, and it has an interesting history. It turns out that every year five thousand participants in our executive program fill out a marketing survey in which they write statements indicating the most important problems they face. One day Lucy Chin, one of our administrators, handed me a document containing all these statements. A content analysis of the data resulted in a list of forty-five pressing problems. The topics ranged from growing a company to managing personal stress. The list covered a wide territory, and I started to see its potential. People in organizations tend to be driven by a very traditional set of problems, but the solutions evolve. I went to my friends at Jossey-Bass to discuss a publishing project. The discussion eventually grew into the University of Michigan Business School Management Series— Innovative Solutions to the Pressing Problems of Business.

The books are independent of each other, but collectively they create a comprehensive set of management tools that cut across all the functional areas of business—from strategy to human resources to finance, accounting, and operations. They draw on the interdisciplinary research of the Michigan faculty. Yet each book is written so a serious manager can read it quickly and act immediately. I think you will find that they are books that will make a significant difference to you and your organization.

Robert E. Quinn, Consulting Editor
M.E. Tracy Distinguished Professor
University of Michigan Business School

Preface

Over the past two decades, many companies have moved sequentially from focusing on quality to focusing on customer satisfaction, and then on loyalty, and then on relationship management as the panacea of the day. These are all important issues, but it is an error to try to address them independently, without regard to their place in a system. They actually form a chain of causes and effects that build on one another and cannot be treated or managed successfully on their own.

Our purpose in writing this book is to help you establish more explicit linkages from quality to customer satisfaction to loyalty, and ultimately to bottom-line financial performance. Future approaches to customer measurement and management cannot be based on simple arguments—it's no longer enough to assert that "quality is free" or that it is less expensive to satisfy and keep customers than to constantly replace them. Upper managers and executives need specific estimates of the payoffs they should expect from increasing quality, satisfaction, and loyalty in specific ways. Setting priorities and allocating resources requires information of this quality. If middle managers or employees in charge of measuring and improving quality and satisfaction are to be of real service to upper management in this regard, they need to be able to supply the kind of data and information by which payoffs can be estimated.

This book is intended for both "enablers" and "doers" in your company. That is, as an executive in charge of improving quality, customer satisfaction, or loyalty, your job may be to enable others to act through training and support. Or as a specialist within the quality, customer assessment, or product and service development areas of the company, your job may be to collect, analyze, or use customer data to improve quality, satisfaction, and retention. Whatever your particular niche, this text will help you take part in creating an integrated customer measurement and management system that will improve your firm's ability to allocate resources and increase profits.

To establish a customer orientation as a core competency of your company, it is important to recruit or train internal specialists to measure and manage quality, satisfaction, and loyalty. The approach that we outline in this book will help you develop these specialists. The ability to observe and talk to customers, formalize survey instruments, analyze and interpret survey data, and use the output to make resource allocation decisions are skills that a truly customer-oriented firm should own for itself.

We help you meet these needs and challenges through a five-stage process for the implementation of such a system:

1. Identifying the purpose
2. Using qualitative research to build what we call the "lens of the customer," a model of the customer's point of view
3. Creating a quality-satisfaction-loyalty survey
4. Converting data into information through state-of-the-art data analysis
5. Proceeding from information to decisions that set priorities for quality improvement

If you are just starting to collect and use customer data, our five-stage process provides a blueprint for success. If you are experienced at measuring and managing customer data, our process integrates your measurement system and leverages its performance.

▪ Acknowledgments

Many people have been critical to our success. At the University of Michigan Business School, we thank Bob Quinn for developing the UMBS Management Series and encouraging us at every step. We thank the Jossey-Bass team for making this project a reality, especially Cedric Crocker and Byron Schneider. Special thanks also to development editors Alan Venable and John Bergez. Their talent and attention to organization and detail in the editing process have taught us a whole new way to communicate.

This book has benefited tremendously from the inclusion of examples that were made possible by two helpful and supportive industry colleagues. We thank Teri Richman, senior vice president for research and industry affairs at the National Association of Convenience Stores (NACS), for allowing us to use the NACS customer satisfaction model, survey, and data throughout the text. We thank Stellan Flodin, senior vice president of quality at the Volvo Car Company (now part of Ford Motor Company), for allowing us to share with you the recent history of Volvo's move toward a customer orientation that is linked to the bottom line.

But most of all we thank our spouses Jill Marie and Lena, the Olsson girls, and our children, Alexander, Andrew, Thomas, Amie, and Samuel. Their love and support keep us going, although Lennart and Ann Mari's crayfish party and the fishing trip helped as well. The result has been an exhausting but thoroughly enjoyable book-writing process.

May 2000

Michael D. Johnson
Ann Arbor, Michigan

Anders Gustafsson
Karlstad, Sweden

To Jill Marie and Lena,
The Olsson girls

Improving Customer Satisfaction, Loyalty, and Profit

Creating a Customer Measurement and Management System

E very company must be able to satisfy and retain customers. That is the key to its business performance. Your job—as an executive in charge of improving quality, customer satisfaction, or loyalty—may be to enable others to act through training and support. Alternatively, if you're in the quality, customer assessment, or development areas of your company, your job may be to do the work directly—to collect, analyze, or use customer data to improve quality, satisfaction, and retention. Whether you are an *enabler* or a *doer*, customer satisfaction and retention are your responsibility. Providing high-quality products and services builds strong relationships with customers and ensures future revenue streams. By giving your customers no reason to switch—and every reason to stay—you insulate them from the competition.

■ Is Your Company Taking a Systems Approach?

Even though you may agree about the importance of customers in driving performance, an important question remains. Does your company align its activities to satisfy and retain customers? Too often the answer is either "no" or "not so well." To help understand the problem, consider how a customer focus has evolved in recent decades.

In the 1970s, quality gurus argued that "quality is free." That is, a tireless pursuit of improvement should not only increase efficiency but also increase customer satisfaction in the process, saving enough on costs and bringing in enough new and repeat business to more than cover any expenditures on quality. This was an underlying concept in the success of many Japanese companies. In the 1980s the experts began to focus more directly on increasing customer satisfaction as an explicit goal. Satisfying and keeping customers, it was argued, is simply less expensive than constantly replacing them. More recently, quality and satisfaction have been viewed as not sufficient by themselves. Companies boast of moving "beyond" quality and satisfaction to focus directly on customer loyalty as the key to profitability.

Yet to argue that quality, or satisfaction, or loyalty is what matters misses the point. These factors form a chain of cause and effect, building on each other so that they cannot be treated separately. They represent a system that must be measured and managed as a whole if you want to maximize results.

An example from our teaching experiences underscores the nature of the problem and why companies need to take a systems approach to customer measurement and management.

Back in 1993 an executive seminar participant from a Fortune 100 company introduced himself as the "customer satisfaction manager" for his organization. This prompted one of the authors to ask, "What happened to the quality manager?" The participant replied that quality was passé, and that customer satisfaction had become the hot topic in his organization. In fact, being the quality manager had become the "kiss of death" from a career standpoint—a dead-end job! Five years later, a seminar participant from the same company introduced himself as the "customer loyalty manager" for the organization. Again the natural question arose, "What happened to the customer satisfaction manager?" "Oh, him?" It turned out that the satisfaction manager was now the one with the dead-end job.

Many business organizations are beginning to recognize the need to avoid this "Book of the Month Club" mentality and to view customers from a systems perspective. They want explicit linkages that extend from internal processes to customer perceptions to customer satisfaction to loyalty—and ultimately to bottom-line performance. The framework in this book will give executives hard numbers and not just persuasive theories to show that the connection is real and that improving satisfaction and loyalty really does improve profits. And those on the front lines—the quality engineers and service providers—will get specific guidance on what to improve and how to improve it to get the optimal response from customers.

This book will show you how to create an integrated customer measurement and management system that will help you allocate resources and increase profits. To create such a system, you must first understand your company's entire system for generating profit, from internal quality through to business performance. A systems approach acts on the basis of collected and interpreted customer data—but then you have to use the data to allocate resources and create change in the system or else you merely waste time and money.

■ Pursuing Success Through Customer Measurement and Management

With an effective customer measurement and management system, you can build organizational value. To do so, you will continually pursue three key activities that underlie a customer orientation: (1) gather customer information, (2) spread that information throughout the organization, and (3) use the information to maintain, improve, or innovate in products and processes.[1]

You need solid information about the concrete product and service attributes or features that customers value, the more abstract consequences and benefits these attributes provide, and ultimately the personal values they serve. The purpose is to understand what your customers want not only in today's products and services but in tomorrow's as well. When you understand your customers at the various levels that motivate their behavior, you can see their present needs and predict their future needs as well.

To maintain a customer orientation throughout your organization, you need to make sure that customer information gets to everyone who is involved—either directly or indirectly—in improving quality and value and satisfying customers. This both prepares the entire organization for change and provides benchmarks by which to monitor its performance. Finally, you need to prime the organization to act on the customer information to improve product and service offerings so as to increase satisfaction, loyalty, and profitability. This makes it essential to clarify the links among these three factors and understand how your company delivers a compelling product to its customers.

Creating a customer measurement and management system is central to the pursuit of all three of these activities. With such a system in place, you have your customer information in a form that can serve as a basis for both incremental and more revolutionary product and service improvements. The system also makes it easier to share customer information throughout an organization, enhancing its ability to follow through on that information to make product and process changes. It is essential to view customer measurement from a systems perspective that encompasses multiple areas of measurement and expertise (from engineering and design through market research and strategy to finance and accounting) so that you pick up both concrete and abstract details—both what the customers like and dislike and why they react that way—and develop information that will be genuinely useful.

Lens of the Customer or Lens of the Organization?

Now you may well be saying, "But we already do a good job of gathering customer information, spreading it, and acting on the voice of the customer." The question is whether you really adopt the "lens of the customer" in this process or fall into the trap of relying on the "lens of the organization."

Figure 1.1 illustrates the difference. The lens of the customer shows you your products and services—and the benefits they provide—from your customers' perspective. You see them as they really are in the marketplace, rather than the different and potentially misleading picture you're likely to get from the lens of your own organization. For example, if you run a convenience store chain you may be inclined to view the chain's stores as providing customers with people (service), products (from soft drinks to gasoline), and operations (such as opening hours), each under the management of a different department or business function (see left side of Figure 1.1). The problem is that customers may not share this perspective. Customers view products and services from the standpoint of the benefits they provide and problems they solve, which may not align well with individual business process areas. In this case, customers are looking for safety, convenience, and cleanliness (see right side of Figure 1.1), which are benefits that are not uniquely provided by specific business process areas. Rather, they cut across the people, products, and operating policies of the stores.

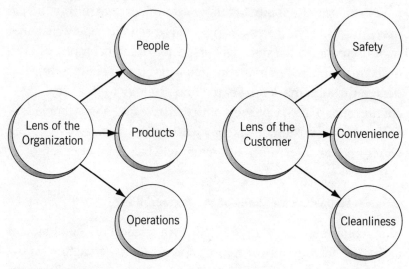

Figure 1.1. Whose Lens Is Best?

Aside from providing a more accurate picture of the drivers of satisfaction and loyalty, adopting the lens of the customer has other advantages. It blurs functional boundaries and provides a common basis and language for communication. The forging of concrete links from area to area within a company is also a key to effective implementation. When an organization reaches a consensus on the importance of customer benefits that are not defined along functional or business process lines, it finds it much easier to engage in the cross-functional activities required to truly innovate and implement change.

Linking Quality to Financial Performance

Figure 1.2 shows our framework for understanding the links from internal quality to financial performance. We emphasize the word *framework* here. Our aim is to show just what links and models are possible. The figure is not a model in itself, it is a basis for developing models. The actual elements and links in any model vary tremendously from company to company and context to context. After describing the framework, we will illustrate this point using two very different cases in which companies (Volvo and Sears) have developed models to become more customer focused.

The framework includes four general areas: internal quality, external quality and satisfaction, customer loyalty and retention, and financial performance. *Internal quality* encompasses various production and maintenance processes. In the case of a manufactured product, it includes everything from manufacturing processes to the physical characteristics and attributes that describe the product. In a service and retailing context, it includes the service offer, the physical surroundings, and the satisfaction of employees and the resulting service quality they provide.

External quality and satisfaction encompasses what customers see in the purchase and consumption experience: the attributes and benefits that products and services provide and the costs they impose, and the conclusions the customers draw about the company. In the area of customer loyalty and retention, *loyalty* is a customer's intention or predisposition to buy, while *retention* is the behavior itself (as when a customer returns to a restaurant, comes back to buy the same brand of car, or purchases another financial instrument from the same institution). Although we will use the term *loyalty* at times to encompass both intended loyalty and actual retention, it is important to understand the distinction. When

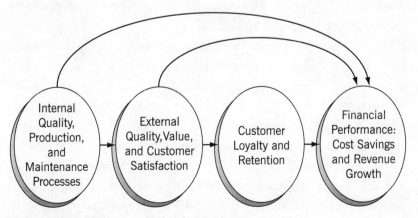

Figure 1.2. A Framework for Linking Quality to Performance

actual retention information is available, it proves extremely valuable in sorting out the drivers of financial performance. When it is unavailable, as it often is, you can use loyalty measures as a proxy for retention.

Quality, satisfaction, and loyalty ultimately affect financial performance, both directly and indirectly. The framework illustrates this point and highlights the possibility that there may be a tension between direct and indirect effects. Consider first the impact of internal quality. Producing a high-quality product or service at an attractive price indirectly affects financial performance through its effect on external customer perceptions of the purchase-consumption experience. But internal quality may also have a direct effect on costs and revenues. According to the "quality is free" argument, improvements in internal quality can increase productivity and lower internal costs and thus directly increase profitability.[2] Recent research suggests, however, that this link is likely to be more positive for products and less positive or even negative for services.[3] Why the difference? Services are produced and delivered at a time and place that is typically dictated by the customer. Thus improving service quality often requires an increase in personnel and operating or contact hours, which raises operating costs.

The external quality, value, and customer satisfaction component of the framework also has both direct and indirect effects on costs and revenues. Indirectly, a positive overall experience predisposes customers to stay loyal toward a product, service, or provider, which generates future sales. Satisfaction thus contributes to financial performance through its effect on loyalty and retention. But satisfaction also has direct effects, independent of loyalty.[4] The cost of maintaining a customer account—or fixing a product—is a direct function of how happy the customer is. Satisfied customers are less likely to demand expensive product repairs or replacements or to invoke service guarantees. Also—even outside the world of TV commercials—people do talk about the products and services they buy, and your company's entry into that stream of word-of-mouth publicity is through perceived quality and satisfaction rather than through loyalty. Satisfaction is *news*—something to talk about—while loyalty is a background state that goes without saying unless something happens to damage it.

The direct effects of loyalty and retention on performance include revenues from repeat purchases, reduction in costs of finding new customers (to replace lost customers), and revenues generated through cross-selling. Another direct effect is the price premium that loyal customers often pay. Because loyal customers are not actively shopping for alternatives, they tend to be insulated from price incentives and offers such as coupons, price cuts, and free merchandise.

How Volvo and Sears Tailored Their Profit Models

The recent turnaround at Volvo Car Company provides a good example of how a durable goods manufacturer views the links described in our framework.[5] In 1991, Volvo was performing poorly in the global automotive market. It ranked as low as twenty-sixth out of thirty-four brands in the J. D. Power Initial Quality Study in the United States, and sales and profitability were suffering. In its comeback effort, Volvo began to develop a customer orientation from a total quality management foundation. Formerly, Volvo had emphasized changing internal quality to improve productivity and reduce costs. Its management realized, however, that just focusing on internal quality was insufficient. Internal improvements had to matter to the customers before they could create improved external quality, customer satisfaction, and loyalty.

This led Volvo's management to adopt the broader model of quality illustrated in Figure 1.3. The left side of the figure emphasizes the direct links from internal quality to improved profitability (via productivity and cost reductions). The right side of

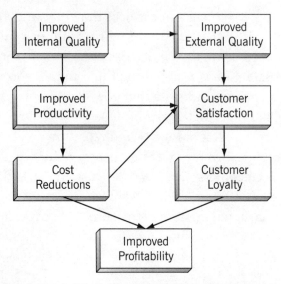

Figure 1.3. Volvo's Model of the Factors That Affect Financial Performance

Source: Adapted from Flodin, S., Nelson, T., and Gustafsson, A. "Improved Customer Satisfaction Is Volvo Priority," in M. D. Johnson, A. Herrmann, F. Huber, and A. Gustafsson (eds.), *Customer Retention in the Automotive Industry: Quality, Satisfaction and Loyalty,* Wiesbaden, Germany: Gabler, 1997, p. 44.

the figure emphasizes the indirect links from internal quality to profitability that run through customer-defined quality, satisfaction, and loyalty. The development of this comprehensive view was fundamental to the changes in policy at Volvo, which we discuss in more detail in Chapter Two. It helped Volvo to outperform twenty-three competitors in the J. D. Power IQS study, reaching third place in 1996. By 1998, the Volvo Car Company had reestablished its quality in the eyes of customers and was among the most profitable automotive producers in Europe. This was a major reason behind its acquisition by Ford Motor Company (other reasons included overcapacity in the global automotive industry and synergies in product lines).

Volvo's approach is just one example of the variety of tailored models that are consistent with the framework in Figure 1.2. Like Volvo, Sears has attempted to radically transform itself into a more customer-focused organization. But since Sears is a retailer that competes primarily on service, its model has evolved quite differently.[6] Internal quality at Sears is primarily about its people and the service they provide. The Sears model draws directly on a service-profit chain that links internal quality (including employee satisfaction and loyalty) to service quality, and the satisfaction generated by service quality to loyalty and financial performance.[7]

Sears's variation on this model is shown in Figure 1.4. Sears learned that employee attitudes about their jobs and the company directly affect employee behavior and retention. Employee behavior, in turn, affects customers' perceptions of the help and merchandise value at Sears stores. These customer perceptions subsequently affect overall satisfaction, word of mouth, loyalty, and profitability.

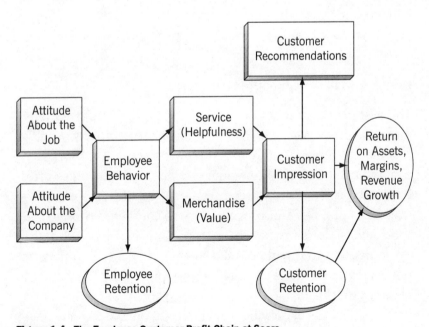

Figure 1.4. The Employee-Customer-Profit Chain at Sears

Source: Adapted from Rucci, A. J., Kirn, S. P., and Quinn, R. T. "The Employee-Customer-Profit Chain at Sears," *Harvard Business Review*, 1998, 76, 82–97; see p. 91.

In developing its model, Sears has discovered both direct effects of satisfaction on financial performance and indirect effects through loyalty, which is consistent with our framework. A quantitative employee-customer-profit model at Sears has helped the company to establish very specific links that have enabled it to improve financial performance. The model shows, for example, that a 5-point improvement in employee attitudes (on a 0 to 100 scale) drives a 1.3-point improvement in customer satisfaction, which in turn drives a 0.5 percent improvement in revenue growth.

The Volvo and Sears models share a common logic, but each model is uniquely tailored to the organization's own situation. Both models link internal quality through to profitability. At the same time, each reflects the nature of a specific company, its customers and offerings, and the contexts involved. When you look at your own company, you will see that the same logic will work for you when you develop a similar understanding of your own customers and what you can offer them.

Moving from Data to Prioritized Decisions

The best measurement system can only provide information—it can't make decisions for you. People make decisions, whether it is the convenience store executive who sets corporate priorities, the front-line service manager who translates these priorities into policies and procedures, or the service worker who translates policies and procedures into concrete actions. At all three levels, decision makers are much more likely to choose to do something that will help the store chain succeed if they understand what matters to customers and how the job at hand can enhance that value.

The process of moving from information to decisions draws heavily on *importance-performance analysis.*[8] According to this analysis, the most cost-effective areas of product and service performance to improve are those that are important to customers *and* on which, at the same time, the company is performing poorly. Executives and managers must identify these priority areas of high importance and low performance. As an output of this selection process, they can categorize and display the drivers of satisfaction and loyalty using a strategic satisfaction matrix like the one in Figure 1.5.[9]

The matrix identifies four categories of performance drivers with different market action implications. Again, the aspects to improve first are those where impact or importance is high and performance is weak. This focuses resources and quality improvement efforts likely to have the greatest impact on satisfaction and thus on loyalty and profitability. Those aspects where performance and impact are both high reflect a firm's competitive advantage. It is essential to maintain if not improve performance on these drivers. When impact and performance are both weak, on the other hand, there is no need to waste resources on improvement.

More interesting is the low impact–strong performance category. This may be an area where resources have been wasted in the past because the benefits and attributes are not important

Low Impact and Strong Performance: Maintain or reduce investment or alter target market	High Impact and Strong Performance: Maintain or improve performance— Competitive advantage
Low Impact and Weak Performance: Inconsequential— Do not waste resources	High Impact and Weak Performance: Focus improvements here—Competitive vulnerability

Figure 1.5. Strategic Satisfaction Matrix

to customers. Alternatively, this category may contain drivers of satisfaction that customers see as basic and necessary—so much a part of the product or service that they ignore it as long as it's there when they want it, like electric power or water on tap. Although such drivers are important in an absolute sense, they have little to no impact on satisfaction because there is little variance in their performance. The danger is that a reduction in performance quality would increase the impact on satisfaction (this danger is often referred to as a "slippery slope"). Another possibility here is to find a new target market segment for the product or service. For example, if the quality of an electrical system is so constant that it has no impact on satisfaction in one application, the system might be used in applications where minor fluctuations in this quality are more important and therefore likely to have a real impact on satisfaction.

There is also a danger that something in this category may become important in the future. For example, few customers considered "environmental friendliness" to be an important factor until recently, but more and more people are beginning to pay attention to this aspect of the goods and services they buy. In a growing variety of fields, companies that predicted the importance of this area and prepared their business accordingly clearly have an advantage over those that did not.

■ A Plan for Creating a Customer Measurement and Management System

The remaining five chapters of the book provide the tools and skills that will help you build a tailored customer measurement and management system. Figure 1.6 presents the model we use to both describe the process and organize subsequent chapters. The circular nature of the process reflects the continuous nature of a customer orientation. Customer needs, competitive offer-

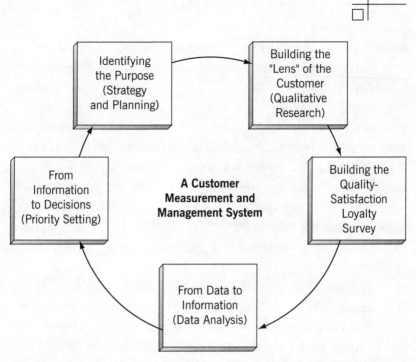

Figure 1.6. A Process Model for Creating a Customer Measurement and Management System

ings, and business technologies change constantly, so customer focus is an ideal of constant growth rather than static achievement. The cycle in Figure 1.6 is thus a continuous process of planning, researching, analyzing, deciding, implementing, and learning.

Chapter Two covers the strategy formulation and planning stage of the system. This includes identifying the system's purpose or goals within a more balanced set of corporate performance measures (including financial goals, employee satisfaction goals, process improvement goals, knowledge and learning goals, and so forth). The chapter explores the key customer and market segmentation issues upon which the system is based, including the distinction between internal and external customers.

Chapter Three tells how to conduct qualitative research to guide the development of the measurement system. Conducting interviews and focus groups and observing customers provides you with the lens through which customers view products and services. This lens is the basis for your quality-satisfaction-loyalty modeling.

Chapter Four tells how to use the lens of the customer to develop a customer monitoring system. It discusses ways to develop and administer surveys that assess the attributes and benefits your products and services provide and the overall levels of customer satisfaction and loyalty that result. The goal is to customize the measurement of quality, value, satisfaction, and loyalty for a particular customer segment, company, and context.

Chapter Five tells how to analyze satisfaction and loyalty data to provide the information you will need to set priorities for improvement. Again, the purpose is to identify both the relative importance and performance of key satisfaction and loyalty drivers. It provides guidelines for identifying the area or areas where importance is high and performance is low, which offer the most potential return on quality improvement efforts. We develop a statistical approach to help you estimate your system or model linking quality to loyalty and financial performance. We also provide concrete examples.

Chapter Six tells how to evaluate system outputs to make decisions. As emphasized earlier, management must take part in categorizing the output of a customer analysis into a strategic satisfaction matrix. Just where boundaries are set between high-versus low-impact drivers and strong versus weak performance depends on a variety of factors, including what you can achieve in the time available, your cost structure, and your overall strategy. Interpreting model outputs also requires appropriate benchmarks for evaluating both performance and importance. We will end Chapter Six by describing how to translate customer priorities into their means of accomplishment.

■ Outsource the Process or Create a Competency?

Who should collect your customer data, analyze it, and use it to set priorities and allocate resources? It often seems logical to delegate the satisfaction and loyalty measurement operation to outside research firms and consultants. This is especially true early in the process of becoming a customer-oriented organization, because outside specialists offer specific skills related to collecting and analyzing customer data that you do not have. Unfortunately, if you delegate the system, your company does not take ownership of it, and you and your people may fail to learn or acquire the skills necessary to measure and manage customer data on your own. The consultant's bills, heavy as they are likely to be, are only a small part of the cost of handing off a customer information system.

Bear in mind that when customer information is the key to strategy, it should reside within the company. Your best teachers about what is right and wrong with your products and services are your own customers. Direct contact with customers and customer data is a critical part of learning what it takes to satisfy customer needs. No matter how good the consultants are, they will always function as filters.

An important part of establishing a customer orientation as a core competency is creating, over time, internal specialists to measure, model, and manage quality, satisfaction, and loyalty. The transformation from relying on external specialists to having your own internal specialists is illustrated in Figure 1.7. Early in the process, external experts are apt to be a necessity. They can provide the interviewing, surveying, data warehousing, statistical analysis, and interpretation skills that you may lack or not yet want (or be able) to invest in. Over time, however, continued reliance on external specialists becomes costly and also fails to develop customer measurement and management as a core

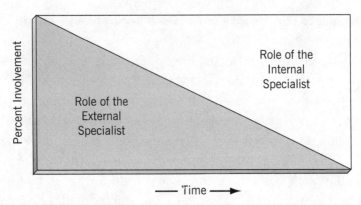

Figure 1.7. Moving from External to Internal Specialists

competency. Internalization of the process allows you to adapt to changing market needs and competitive environments in a cost-effective fashion. More important, your organization accepts ownership of the process and the data—and the decisions that emerge.

This is not to say that all parts of the process should be brought in-house in all cases. You may not want to try to run a survey that involves computer-aided telephone interviews or a Web-based system with highly specialized personnel (such as trained interviewers) and potential economies of scale. Even in the most customer-savvy organization, it may be best to outsource certain parts of the process. At the same time, a truly customer-oriented firm should own rather than rent the ability to observe and to talk to customers, formalize survey instruments, analyze and interpret customer data, and use the output to make resource allocation decisions.

CHAPTER SUMMARY

Over the last three decades business organizations have evolved from a focus on quality to a focus on customer satisfaction, and onward to a focus on loyalty as a means of creating value. A customer measurement and management system views each of these areas as an indispensable link in a chain of causes and effects that runs from internal quality through to profitability. The goal of this book is to help you and your organization create an integrated customer measurement and management system for making effective resource allocation decisions and increasing profitability. In the process of building a system, organizations develop internal specialists capable of gathering, analyzing, and interpreting customer data. Truly customer-oriented companies should, over time, add these skills to their core competencies.

A systems approach to customer measurement and management also requires that you tailor the system to your unique purpose, customers, and contexts. As an illustration, Volvo's model incorporates the positive effects of improving internal quality on both productivity and customer perceptions of quality, satisfaction, and loyalty. In contrast, a major retailer such as Sears incorporates the central role that satisfied employees play in delivering quality and value to customers.

These measurement systems and models are not substitutes for decision making. Rather, they provide the information you need to make resource allocation decisions and manage the process. The system provides information on how the company and its competitors are performing in different areas and how important the areas are to customers.

When combined with cost and strategy considerations, the system allows both enablers and doers to create organizational value through a continuous focus on customers. To maximize the value generated by the system, make sure your company's own staff perform the bulk of the work of collecting and interpreting customer data, so that you get the full benefit of the insights generated by the effort.

Questions to Consider

1. What role do customers play in driving your company's financial performance?
2. Evaluate the systems and methods that you currently use to measure and manage customer data. Do they reflect the lens of the customer or the lens of the organization?
3. Whose job is it to gather, understand, and disseminate your customer data? Whose job should it be?

Strategy and Planning

Before you dive in and start conducting customer interviews or surveys, you must know how your measurement system will be used. This chapter focuses on the strategy and planning for such a system. Since a customer orientation builds on internal quality, we'll start with a brief overview of quality management and its role in driving company strategy and customer measures. We'll then discuss two related approaches to translating strategy into action: policy deployment and balanced performance measures. Then we'll focus on the process of getting started on developing a customer measurement and management system—or improving an existing one—which involves taking a look at the breadth and depth of the proposed system and the role of market segmentation in it.

■ Build on a Quality Foundation

In our customer satisfaction framework, internal quality is the first in the chain of events that drives financial performance.[1] It's important not to underestimate the role of *total quality management* (or TQM, also known as *company-wide quality management*, CWQM, and as *total quality control*, TQC)—nor to exaggerate it.[2] For long-term survival, businesses have been forced to improve their abilities to change and innovate. But internal quality management is not in itself sufficient to assure success. Internal quality improvements must be linked to improvements in external quality, satisfaction, loyalty, and financial performance. And the links must be established in an environment of constantly evolving customer preferences, markets, competitors, and technologies.

The broad principles and methods of quality management apply directly to the development of a customer measurement system. The concept of quality should unify all of a company's activities. After all, only your customers can ultimately define quality for you! In the end, it doesn't matter how well the production system works, how well marketing functions are performed, or how good the company's strategy is. If no one buys, there will be no revenues.

Quality experts emphasize three basic strategies for successful quality management: use reference models or benchmarks, set priorities for quality improvement, and focus your resources.[3]

Benchmark Process and Output

Do not try to do things completely on your own. Instead, make use of reference models or benchmarks when they're available.

Benchmarking is particularly important in developing a customer measurement and management system.

Process benchmarking—finding out how things are done—works as well in developing a customer measurement and management system as in any other area of business. When you can manage it, arrange visits to firms with strong reputations to gauge their practices and learn what they are doing, see how they are doing it, and understand what is possible. Devote some time to reverse engineering their products as well.[4] And don't limit the benchmarking to competitors—in a general area such as customer measurement, you'll find individuals or organizations in many fields who excel in areas that you are interested in improving. Benchmarking on their processes can help you to learn how to conduct better customer interviews, develop and administer more effective surveys, and analyze customer data in more productive ways—and they're likely to be much more willing to share information with you if you're not trying to sell the same offering to the same customers.

For *output* or *performance benchmarking,* you will measure your product or service against direct or indirect competitors on various dimensions such as internal or technical quality, external or perceived quality and value, and overall customer satisfaction, loyalty, and retention. As noted in Chapter Six, external benchmarks will help you interpret your findings regarding your own customers and decide just where to devote your resources to get the most mileage from your improvement efforts.

Set Priorities for Quality Improvement

The second basic strategy of quality management is the universal law of priorities. In a quality context, it is often said that 20 percent of parts, processes, or people account for 80 percent of quality problems (often called the *Pareto principle*). Each customer and each market will react differently to the various drivers of satisfaction and loyalty, so one of your primary goals in customer measurement is to identify the drivers that are most important to improve. As described in Chapter One, you need to find out where the impact on customers is high and your current performance is poor. Your goal should be to set priorities and *optimize* rather than *maximize* your quality and satisfaction improvement efforts.

Focus Your Resources

Once you have chosen the area or areas to change, the third basic strategy of quality management is to concentrate your resources to maximal effect. The goal is to create a company-wide focus on the things that matter most for performance and survival. This is one of the most important yet also most often neglected aspects of quality management. Increasingly, managers face a common problem in that their customer measurement systems point out specific needs for improvement, but their organizations don't respond. The manager knows what area or areas to attack, but has difficulty getting anyone to do anything about it. This is where the lens of the customer shows its usefulness. Once the concept spreads through an organization the independent actions of each individual and department are much more likely to fit into the overall improvement effort.

■ Two Ways to Translate Strategy into Action

Since no amount of information will do you any good if no one will act on it, creating an environment where resources get focused on quality management is in many ways the key element of the process. One basic approach to this problem, called *policy deployment*, has proven very effective where a company has a clear priority regarding what policy to deploy. A variation known as *balanced performance measures* allows a company to determine and deploy a balanced mix of quality improvements.

Customer Policy Deployment

Policy deployment, or hoshin planning *(hoshin kanri)* as it is sometimes called, is a powerful quality management process that converts a company's strategy into operational change and effectively moves different units within the company in the same direction.[5] Customer policy deployment, in particular, aims to move the entire organization to focus more on customers in order to increase their satisfaction and loyalty. Policy deployment includes four major steps:

1. *Mission and Vision:* Clearly state the organization's philosophy, mission, and vision (also called the *president's diagnosis*).
2. *Goals:* Understand exactly where the organization is today and where it wants to be in the short, medium, and long term with regard to specific criteria or goals.
3. *Communication Strategy:* Communicate the mission, vision, and goals throughout the organization.
4. *Priority Setting and Implementation:* Set priorities, align the incentives, and implement quality improvement projects accordingly (using project management).

The turnarounds at Volvo and Sears, introduced in Chapter One, illustrate different applications of the customer policy deployment process.

Customer Policy Deployment at Volvo

Making customers a priority became a strategy for Volvo's survival in the intensely competitive global automotive industry. Back in 1991, the question was how to create a customer orientation in a traditionally engineering-driven company. Volvo quickly realized that policy deployment was a natural means of building on its quality management foundations to move the company from an engineering focus to a customer focus. Here is a summary of how Volvo implemented the four major phases of policy deployment:[6]

- *Volvo's Mission and Vision:* "To be the world's most desired and successful premium car brand."
- *Volvo's Goals:* "To be number 5 in customer satisfaction (according to the J. D. Power IQS study) in 1995 and number 3 in 1997."
- *Volvo's Communication Strategy:* Stop keeping secrets about customer complaints; give employees an open information system and a broad view of the customer value-added process that encompasses the vehicle sales and service experience throughout the life of the vehicle.
- *Volvo's Priority Setting and Implementation:* Use quality teams to focus on the two hundred highest-priority areas (out of two thousand possibilities identified in an initial review), and reward team members based on the degree to which Volvo met its corporate goals as well as on the degree to which the team met its own goals.

Once mission statements work their way through various levels of management, they often end up reading like the Boy Scouts' oath. Companies want to be all things to all people. In contrast, Volvo's vision was specifically to be the most desired successful specialty car brand. While abstract and forward-looking, the vision nonetheless pointed to a particular segment of the automotive market in which Volvo wanted to excel. Quantitatively, Volvo's goal was defined in terms of placement in a specific independent survey—to be number 5 in its industry by 1995 and number 3 by 1997. Although any measurement system has its strengths and weaknesses, by defining customer satisfaction using the J. D. Power IQS study, Volvo effectively defined where it was (twenty-sixth out of thirty-four makes) and where it wanted to be at different points in time. Volvo effectively aligned its mission and vision to concrete measures and goals.

Volvo's next step was communication. Stellan Flodin, the senior vice president in charge of quality, and Jan-Olof Nilsson, senior vice president of Business Area 900, led the effort to create a communication process and culture of openness across the company. Volvo abandoned its hush-hush approach to quality and customer data in favor of a more open system in which information was made available to anyone who could influence customer satisfaction. This was critically important at Volvo because its employees perceived their company as doing quite well. Internally, they had been improving products and processes from year to year all along. But externally, relative quality was falling and the company was losing ground to competitors. This decline was a well-kept secret until Volvo decided to change policy and speak freely about its problems.

Many of the problems reported in the IQS studies involved customers' experiences with sales and service, so it was essential that Volvo encompass the entire value-added chain (from production to delivery and dealer service) in its policy deployment process. Over a period of about two years, the company created an environment in which individuals from very different value-adding areas worked together to solve a variety of customer problems. Reported quality problems came to be viewed as opportunities to learn and improve rather than as negative reflections on any particular area, team, or individual.

As noted, Volvo's customer data revealed over two thousand areas in which quality improvements might be made. The final stage of the process, project management, set priorities and put quality teams to work improving approximately two hundred of the most glaring problem areas. On the Volvo 850, for example, customer data revealed that the manual transmission alone generated a surprising number of complaints (about twenty per hundred vehicles). For example, many customers said the manual gear box was too stiff, and people of below-average height added that the stick shift was too far away and difficult to reach in some gears. A project team was therefore deployed to improve the quality of the transmission.[7] Additional customer surveys allowed the team to translate customer perceptions into design and part changes that, when introduced, decreased the incidence of complaints by over 50 percent.

A key to making all this happen, however, was that Volvo aligned the project teams' and individuals' goals with overall policy goals. Team members were compensated based on whether their teams met project goals (such as reducing transmission problems per hundred cars from twenty to ten to five over time) and whether Volvo met its overall corporate goals (such as reducing overall problems per hundred cars to reach the number 5 position by 1995 and the number 3 position by 1997).

Customer Policy Deployment at Sears
The policy deployment process that Sears is using to create a customer focus is similar to the process at Volvo. The main difference is that, whereas Volvo built on its knowledge of quality management to implement policy deployment from the top down, Sears is using the development of its employee-customer-profit chain (the idea that satisfied employees make for satisfied customers and thereby increase sales and profits, described in Chapter One) to drive the deployment process from the bottom up.[8] The process has been more implicit than explicit.

Retail-service companies have not gone through the same quality management revolution and training as manufacturing companies such as Volvo. But once Sears's employee-customer-profit chain was developed, it became an important tool to drive change in the company's mission, vision, goals, and communication. Everyone from senior managers to store employees had to be taught the logic of the model and its implications, including how the company's competitive environment had changed. The company held town hall meetings and used learning maps to help employees grasp the logic behind the model so that they, in turn, could apply it at the store level. In the end, the deployment process has helped build a leadership model that incorporates the various aspects of the employee-customer-profit chain. The leadership model is to make Sears a compelling place to work, shop, and invest.

Yet the deployment process has progressed more slowly at Sears than at Volvo. The process at Sears has been more data driven, working from the bottom up. Only after the employee-customer-profit chain was developed did Sears executives confront many of the challenges in deploying policy, from a lack of buy-in among top executives to communication problems among their retail employees. And arguably, Volvo has been more successful at implementing its customer orientation and turning the corner on profitability. After some initial success, financial performance at Sears remains weak.[9]

■

These results aren't surprising, and they provide a useful warning to those in service industries. Product companies tend to have a history of quality management when they begin to implement customer policy deployment, and this gives them a strong head start. Few service companies have gone through the same quality revolution, although there are important exceptions. Disney, Fidelity Investments, and USAA, for example, have long-standing commitments to quality management and its principles. (Disney has used policy deployment in the development of its theme parks for many years.) But most service firms simply did not get the wake-up call that hit manufacturing firms in the 1970s and 1980s, when they were confronted with competitors producing higher-quality products in less time and at lower cost.[10]

If you manage or work in a service industry such as telecommunication, insurance, or banking, very likely your company is now experiencing or will soon experience the same type of global competition and cost pressures as your counterparts in the manufacturing world. Technology such as the Internet now provides a basis for delivering cost-effective global service. The warning from product companies is clear. If you hope to continue to prosper, establish a culture that emphasizes quality as your foundation for using customer information to drive organizational change.

Balanced Performance Measures

Balanced performance measures or BPMs share many of the principles of policy deployment. But whereas policy deployment has always been an explicit means of translating strategy into action, BPMs were initially developed as a way of balancing the needs of multiple stakeholders in an organization. Rather than focusing mainly on customers, BPMs recognize that a customer focus must be balanced against the needs of other stakeholders, such as owners, employees, and suppliers. A popular approach to developing BPMs is the balanced scorecard, which is illustrated in Figure 2.1.[11]

Companies use the balanced scorecard to assess their performance and strategy in a highly integrated fashion. The scorecard's four main components are the company's financial perspective, the customer perspective, the internal business process perspective, and the learning and innovation perspec-

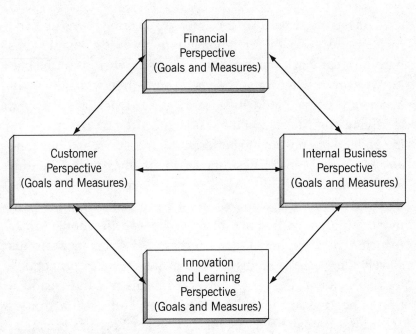

Figure 2.1. The Balanced Scorecard
Adapted from Robert S. Kaplan and David P. Norton, "The Balanced Scorecard—Measures That Drive Performance," *Harvard Business Review*, 70 (January-February, 1992), p. 72.

tive. The *customer perspective* includes those customer measures that are most important for the company to improve, such as targets for customer satisfaction or account penetration. The *financial perspective* includes targets the company sets with respect to both financial (market value) and accounting (revenue and profit) measures. The *internal perspective* includes internal quality and business process measures, such as the number of hours the company spends talking with customers about current or future projects, or the level of employee satisfaction. The *innovation and learning perspective* include goals and measures for investments in training and new product or service development. For each perspective, goals and measures are developed and drilled down to operational levels for teams and individuals ("personal scorecards").

As balanced performance measurement systems evolved through the 1990s, their relationship to policy deployment has become clear. For example, in more recent versions of the balanced scorecard, a company's vision and strategy drive a management process that includes strategy feedback and learning, clarifying and translating the vision and strategy, communicating and linking rewards to performance measures, and planning and setting targets.[12] These stages obviously parallel the four main steps in policy deployment described earlier. Yet important differences remain. Whereas a full policy deployment moves an organization in a completely new direction, such as focusing more explicitly on customers, BPMs balance various stakeholders' needs. In this sense, BPMs are a weak form of policy deployment. They more or less presume that the organization is headed in the right direction and align its activities accordingly. A balanced scorecard approach keeps an organization on course through an integrated management and budgeting process.

BPMs also lack any guiding framework or model of the drivers of financial performance. The approach focuses generally on synergies among the various perspectives or stakeholder needs. As emphasized in Chapter One, it is important that you build your measurement system on an evolving understanding of the drivers of financial performance that is tailored to your company and competitive environment, as Volvo and Sears did.

Although this book's focus is primarily on the customer perspective, balanced performance measures do serve as a reminder that the measurement and management process described here can be applied to other stakeholders as well. In the Sears model, for example, employee attitudes and beliefs are critically important in driving employee behavior. The processes and tools described in this book for developing the lens of the customer can certainly be applied to develop the lens of the employee, supplier, or equity stakeholder as a basis for developing and administering surveys, analyzing data, and setting priorities for improvement.

■ Breadth and Depth of a Customer Measurement and Management System

When you embark on a strategy of customer-driven quality improvement, questions will arise about how to set up a system to collect the data you need to work with. Many of these questions can be broadly categorized as relating either to *system breadth*—the range of internal and external customers and market segments that you want to measure—or to *system depth*—the level of detail and nature of the information that you gather.

System Breadth and Types of Customers

Companies typically serve a range of very different customers both inside and outside the organization. Internal customers may be in the same physical location, as when marketing and finance are customers of information services, or in different locations, as when manufacturing plants are customers of the home office. External customers range from wholesalers and retailers to end users. The customer chain in Figure 2.2 shows three levels of customers: plant customers, retailing customers, and end users. We have kept this example simple to make the relationships easy to see on paper; in practice any given organization or network is likely to have a much larger number of customer levels, as any

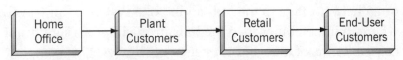

Figure 2.2. A Simple Internal-to-External Customer Chain

individual might be considered someone else's customer. And it isn't enough to track exchanges of funds for goods or services, as even external customers don't necessarily pay to assume that role—regulatory agencies are customers for reports, for example, and people downstream (literally or metaphorically) from traditional end users are the ones likely to be customers for ecological and recycling efforts.

To determine just which customers should be your primary measurement and management focus, refer back to the framework in Chapter One. What links in the customer chain drive your financial performance? Where are the links from quality to satisfaction to loyalty and profitability the strongest? Those are the places where you're likely to get the most mileage out of any investment in improved quality. Even without a detailed measurement system, you probably have some knowledge or understanding of where to start looking.

Think about the nature of the competition and customer choice at each level. The logic of a customer orientation (the idea that quality, satisfaction, and loyalty drive profitability) is based on two critical assumptions. First, the customer is relatively free to choose products and services. This assumption holds for most industries in the developed world today—customers face a dizzying variety of brands of cars, soap, phone service, and most necessities and luxuries, and if one alternative doesn't satisfy there's always another to try. This assumption doesn't always hold true, however—when customers face significant switching costs in moving from one provider to another, or there is only one supplier available, they are essentially hostages.[13] That is, when it's expensive or difficult to find another supplier, only a very dissatisfied customer will switch to a competitor. Airline customers are often held hostage to the hub-and-spoke system of air travel, where flying on other than the hub airline imposes significant costs in terms of time and convenience. However, no company can count on keeping its customers hostage indefinitely. In the gas and electric supply business, for example, many customers still have few options to choose from—but recent deregulation means that the situation is changing rapidly, and customer satisfaction and loyalty are likely to become drivers of profitability soon.

The second important assumption in the logic of a customer orientation is that the important customers are the ones who will generate new business if they're satisfied with their experience—buy replacements for past purchases, buy new offerings, or inspire potential customers to try the company's wares. Investments to satisfy more transient or one-time customers may not generate future revenues or cost savings. The benefits of increasing satisfaction are thus greatest at the level in the customer chain where your customers have both a choice and a potential to reward you with future revenues at lower costs.

Related to the notion of customer choice is the relative *push* versus *pull* of your products and services through the customer chain. Consider a service provider such as Fidelity, which places investment instruments through a variety of independent retailers. In one region, the end users—the individual investors— may have strong brand attitudes and perceptions that have been created over a long period of time through experience, advertising, and word of mouth. In this case, the most important customer in the chain is probably the end user who goes to a retailer (whether an agency or a Web site) in search of a particular offering. The choice in this case resides primarily with end users who pull the product through the chain. Although all customers are important at some level, relatively speaking, the satisfaction of the retailer is not as critical in this case as the satisfaction of the end user. To satisfy and retain their own customers, the retailers need to make the Fidelity offerings available to them.

Elsewhere, investors may be much more likely to follow the advice of the retailer about which brand to purchase. The retailer may be more established and trusted in the end user's mind than any individual brand. If investors are more likely to defer their choice to a trusted retailer, Fidelity is in a position of pushing the product or service through the chain. In this case, the most important thing to measure and manage may be the satisfaction of the retailer and its willingness to push the brand on to the end user. The same logic applies regardless of the product or service—if the offering is seen as interchangeable at the end-user level, you have to give the retailer a reason to favor your brand over others.

Pay Attention to Market Segmentation

At each level in the customer chain, the market segmentation scheme is the key element in your strategic market plan to build a customer measurement system. Market segmentation is the process of identifying and targeting unique populations or *segments* of customers and developing tailored marketing strategies to meet the individual segment needs. To identify and target segments, take the following steps:[14]

1. Group customers into segments based on customer needs, benefits sought, or personal values served.
2. Identify or describe the segments according to their behaviors, lifestyles, or demographics.
3. Evaluate the attractiveness of each segment in terms of, for example, profit potential, risk, capacity utilization, and core competencies required to serve the segment.
4. Determine strategically which segments to target and pursue and, as a result, which segments to measure, analyze, and manage separately.

These steps bring you to a framework for just which customers to measure, analyze, and monitor.[15] Because the drivers of satisfaction and loyalty may be very different from segment to segment, be wary of averaging across segments. Averages can be deceiving. If customer data are aggregated too highly, they provide a profile of an average customer who simply does not exist. If the segments are different enough, they will require separate survey development and analysis. Even when the same survey is applicable to more than one group of customers, be sure to analyze importance and performance levels separately for each group.

Segmentation in a Hotel Chain
Consider, for example, the needs of business customers and vacation customers at "Wolverine Inns" (a fictitious name for a major mid-priced hotel chain we worked with recently). The chain recently segmented its franchisees according to which segment of customers they are most likely to serve, based on the idea that downtown properties cater more to the business customer segment and leisure-area properties cater more to the vacation customer segment.

Figure 2.3 shows the impact-performance matrix for each property type. The matrices are used to set priorities for quality improvement. The company's satisfaction and loyalty survey covers eight general quality areas or customer benefits (reservation process, staff, facilities, grounds, bathroom, room, breakfast, and perceived value) and each area is rated on a variety of attributes. For the moment, just look at the impact and performance aspects of the eight types of benefit. (Chapter Five will take up the issue of setting priorities among the attributes that provide each benefit, such as the friendliness, helpfulness, efficiency, and grooming and appearance of the hotel staff.)

The vertical axes in the figures show how each type of property performs on each of the eight benefits using a weighted average of customers' attribute ratings (on a scale where 1 is poor and 5 is excellent). Both downtown and leisure-area properties, for example, perform very well on the quality of the reservations process. The horizontal axes show the relative importance of each benefit as revealed by its statistical impact on overall satisfaction.

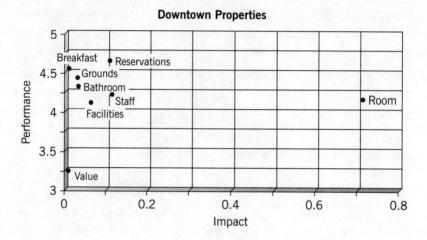

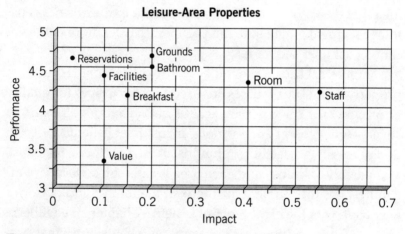

Figure 2.3. Impact-Performance Analysis for Two Hotel Types

For example, the impact score of .75 for quality of the room for the downtown properties shows that as room quality increases by 10 percent, satisfaction increases by 7.5 percent (10 percent × .75). (This example is based on standardized scale values.)

The results reveal vast differences in the drivers of satisfaction across the two property types. Business customers who frequent downtown Wolverine Inn locations look for the hotel to simply provide a clean and comfortable room. They use the hotel for a place to get a good night's sleep and have little interest in its other services. In contrast, a much wider variety of factors drive satisfaction for the vacation customers who frequent the chain's leisure-area properties. The quality of the room is secondary to the quality of service and advice that the staff provides. The quality of the grounds, bathroom, and breakfast are also more important for the vacation customer.

As hotel manager at any given property, you would certainly want to know impact and performance levels for your target customers. Assuming the charts in Figure 2.3 described results for individual hotels, the downtown manager would see improving the quality of the rooms as the greatest priority, given its high impact and currently moderate performance. In contrast, the manager of the leisure-area property would see improving the quality of the staff as relatively more important. Neither manager would have much incentive to do anything about perceived value—the customers' view of the price they are paying for the experience—even though it is far and away the lowest performance area in both cases, because the survey results show that neither group of customers cares much about it. Lowering prices would be costly for the hotel and would make it more difficult to sustain improvements in areas that matter to the customers, so it's best to avoid this step unless the hotel has an incentive to change its customer base to one that regards the current price level as a barrier rather than a minor irritant.

System Depth and Degree of Change

After deciding which customer levels to include in the measurement system and what customers or market segments to include, the next step is to ask what level of generality or detail about the lens of the customer the system should contain. Customer satisfaction is a complex matter, made up of the way the customer perceives the concrete attributes of a product, the benefits the customer derives from those attributes, and the personal values that the product supports.[16] All these elements reside with the customer and are beyond the company's direct control, so we refer to them as *external quality factors.* Measurement systems vary in the amount of detail they provide about external factors such as these.

For example, macro-level measurement systems such as the American Customer Satisfaction Index (ACSI)[17] only include very general differences in external perceptions of overall quality and value as drivers of satisfaction and loyalty. Quality is itself measured using customer ratings of the levels of customization and reliability provided, while value is measured using customer perceptions of the price or prices paid for the quality received. The purpose of measurement systems such as the ACSI is, however, to provide quality, value, satisfaction, and loyalty benchmarks across a very wide range of firms, industry groupings (including products, services, retailers, and government and public agencies), and even countries.[18] Such broad-based comparisons require a measurement system that emphasizes generality and comparability as opposed to depth and detail.

If your goal is to improve or radically reinvent goods and services, you'll need a more detailed and comprehensive information system. It should include information on the range of concrete attributes and abstract benefits that might drive satisfaction and require improvement. Chapter Three will return to the convenience store example and discuss perceived convenience, merchandise quality, and safety as just three of the benefits that directly affect customer satisfaction.

In subsequent chapters we will discuss how to develop these more detailed or in-depth measurement systems for the purpose of measuring and managing customer data for a particular product or service and market segment. Remember that the information in the measurement system is designed to leverage either incremental (evolutionary) or innovative (revolutionary) activities, or both. For example, when Volvo discovered that its customers found its manual transmissions difficult to shift (an attribute-level problem), it translated the problem into one of changing certain parts that immediately reduced complaints.[19] In contrast, when product or service designers are pursuing major innovations, they shift upward from the attribute level to more abstract customer benefits and personal values as input to the design process. Developing a fuel cell or electric vehicle, for example, requires matching the benefits and consequences that the new technology provides (such as zero emissions and moderate performance) with the benefits and values that are important to target customers (such as a willingness to trade off vehicle performance for environmental impact). Product or service design is then a process of developing a whole new configuration of product and service attributes to better serve customer needs.

Revolution or Evolution?
We are often asked when to engage in revolutionary innovation rather than more evolutionary continuous improvement. The key, of course, is to avoid focusing on one to the exclusion of the other, but rather to balance both activities. Masaaki Imai, who was instrumental in developing the *kaizen* or continuous improvement process, emphasizes the importance of maintaining a balance among three activities: maintaining the quality of existing products, services, or processes; achieving kaizen or

continuous improvement; and achieving innovation.[20] The temptation, Imai argues, is to focus only on innovation as a means of making rapid changes and leapfrogging the competition. This ignores the long-term benefits that continuous improvement brings to a company.

When all three activities are balanced, the result is a formidable competitive advantage. Disney is a great example of an organization that consistently manages to balance all three activities.[21] The regular development of new characters for use in movies, television shows, and theme parks is a constant source of innovation. At the same time, Disney works to maintain or keep improving every stage of its customers' experience. The combination has created a legendary service organization that is built on a quality foundation *and* reinvents itself on a regular basis.

How Often to Measure?

Measuring quality, customer satisfaction, and loyalty should be an ongoing, repetitive process. It is difficult, however, to make general recommendations about just how frequently to measure. The frequency varies from company to company and depends on the audience, the stability or volatility of the product or service, and the nature of the market. For instance, if you have relatively few customers it may not be desirable to survey them too often. Needless to say, your customers should never feel that the process is burdensome. And once you do a survey and set some priorities, be sure to implement the changes before you launch another survey. Otherwise, your customers will ask the obvious question: "Why should I bother filling out this survey when you didn't pay any attention to the last one?"

A product's life cycle also affects the frequency of measurement. You need frequent contact with customers early on, when the market is evolving and changes to the product or service can have a great impact on a company's success. Consider the battle between Ericsson and Nokia in the cellular phone market. The early adopters of cellular phones were businesspeople. They simply wanted a reliable phone, which gave Ericsson the edge. But Ericsson did not keep up with the evolution of customer needs in the market and emergence of new market segments that demanded more features and design improvements. This allowed Nokia to achieve a greater advantage as the market evolved.

Later in a product's life cycle, customers are much harder to attract, more valuable to keep, and more costly to lose, so again you want close and frequent customer contacts. And, of course, it is always important to listen carefully to customers when the threat of competition has increased. The general point is that contact with customers should become more frequent during certain critical stages of the product life cycle and market dynamics.

Keeping these contingencies in mind, we recommend a customer satisfaction survey at least yearly. More frequent surveys are likely to have little effect on your improvement efforts when the product and the market are stable. If competition is really active and is moving quickly in a market, it may be necessary to carry out more frequent studies—perhaps even on a quarterly basis. But make sure you have enough resources to process and implement the findings, or the efforts are wasted. It is often a good compromise to measure every six months in times of change.

Finally, remember that there's a difference between customer measures and surveys as the basis of a measurement and management system and more informal surveys or methods designed to take a quick pulse or to identify problems as they occur. The latter methods typically focus on the most recent episode or transaction with a customer (such as the latest stay at the hotel or visit to the bookstore), and are often loosely structured (an informal interview by the manager or an open-ended "opinion" card). Their value toward allocating resources and deciding strategy is limited. At the same time, they may be a valuable source of information for service managers or front-line service personnel to catch and resolve certain classes of problems as they occur.

CHAPTER SUMMARY

Providing external quality and customer satisfaction depends directly on the quality of your company's internal processes, operating policies, strategies, and plans. Whether your company provides products or services (or both), quality management provides a solid foundation for developing and deploying strategy and measuring quality through the lens of the customer. As you move through subsequent chapters, you will see the three basic strategies of quality management. We will describe the use of reference models or benchmarks to interpret and analyze customer data. We will show you how to optimize rather than maximize customer satisfaction and loyalty by setting priorities for quality improvement. Finally, we will describe ways to maximize use of available resources to implement the change. Policy deployment and its variants, including balanced performance measures, are important tools for creating a more universal and consistent focus. These approaches provide companies with a means of translating their customer strategies into action.

Just where to begin building the system requires decisions regarding which customers to include, or system breadth, and how much detail to provide, or system depth. You want to include the kinds of customers that drive business performance. To do this, you will need to ask "which of our internal or external customers are both a source of future profits and have a choice about where they take their business?" To drive profitability, produce and deliver high-quality products and services to satisfy and retain these customers.

When including customers in the measurement system, remember that customers do not all value the same things and behave in the same way. Build your customer measurement systems on an understanding of how your customer base at any given level (such as retail or end-user) is segmented. Segmentation is a process of identifying individuals or populations of customers with unique needs and wants. By paying attention to segment differences you will avoid the pitfall of setting priorities based on "average" customers who don't exist.

In your planning process, also consider just how much detail you will need to measure and how you will use your measurement system. At a general level, macro-level customer measurement systems provide for broad-based comparisons and benchmarking but give only general guidance about what companies should improve (such as product or service quality or value). In this book, the focus is on measurement systems that are more specific to the company or segment; they provide detailed information regarding concrete product or service attributes as well as information about more abstract consequences and benefits. By continually improving the concrete attributes of existing offerings and finding completely new ways to provide customer benefits, you can leverage your customer data to create a truly exemplary level of performance and competitive advantage.

Questions for Consideration

1. How strongly are quality management principles ingrained in your company's culture and day-to-day activities?
2. Does your company need to focus more directly on customers, as through customer policy deployment? Are customer goals properly balanced vis-à-vis other stakeholder needs?
3. In developing or improving your customer measurement systems, how strong is the market strategy and segmentation scheme on which you build? What level of detail and frequency of measurement is appropriate?

Building the Lens of the Customer

To link internal quality to profitability, you have to find out how customers see the products and services they purchase and consume. Your first step (and the subject of this chapter) will be to develop a model of how customers view your firm's products, services, and activities—the "lens of the customer" that will guide the rest of your efforts.

■ Designing a Lens

As discussed in Chapter One, people inside an organization too often develop customer surveys from their own perspective, or how they believe customers view their products and services.

The result is a survey or measurement instrument that embodies the lens of the organization rather than the lens of the customer. You'll often see airline surveys organized in this fashion, for example, full of questions broken out by organizational activity (check-in, preflight service, food and beverage, flight crews, and cabin environment).[1] A survey that aligns question areas with organizational responsibility in this fashion does have the advantage of producing recommendations that are fairly straightforward to implement. If the survey results and priority-setting process indicate that flight crews are most in need of improvement, then the responsibility for making improvements within the organization is clear.

Unfortunately, this type of survey may warp or entirely miss issues that cross organizational boundaries, as when flight crews get blamed for being short-tempered about carry-on baggage that should never have been allowed into the cabin in the first place. Customers tend to form opinions regarding such benefits as service, convenience, and safety that cut across the functional areas of an organization. It is essential, therefore, that the measurement system be based squarely on the lens of the customer. In addition, having a survey instrument that better captures the customers' perception of the company makes the data easier to analyze. We are able to explain more variation in key customer evaluations and behaviors, such as satisfaction and loyalty, when the questionnaire is based on the customers' view. For an airline, such a questionnaire might address a whole range of activities from seat reservations through boarding to baggage claim under the heading of convenience, and everything from the gate lobby staff to the seat cushions under the heading of comfort.

■ The Basic Model

The concrete attributes of a product or service and the abstract benefits it generates occupy different levels in the customers' lens. This distinction is very useful but may take some getting used to, so Figure 3.1 illustrates how it works.

The rectangular objects at the left-hand side of the figure represent the concrete aspects or dimensions on which customers can readily report performance via survey measures (such as whether a sales staff keeps its appointments and returns telephone calls and e-mail messages). The circular objects to the right of the attributes represent the relatively abstract or *latent* variables that capture the benefits or consequences that the attributes provide or, at an even more abstract level, the personal values that they serve. For simplicity, we will refer to all the abstract drivers of satisfaction and loyalty as *benefits*.

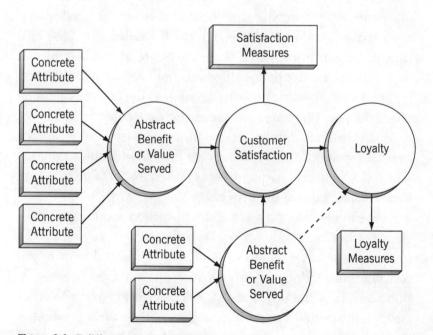

Figure 3.1. **Building the Lens of the Customer**

As in a traditional marketing perspective, the customer satisfaction model embodies the view that products and services compete primarily on the benefits they provide or the needs they fulfill.[2] The concrete attributes of the product or service are only the means to these more abstract ends. Letters, e-mail messages, and faxes all, for example, provide the benefit of communication. You can thus view benefits as the primary drivers of satisfaction in the lens. Notice, however, that benefits may be measured using different numbers of concrete attributes.

Satisfaction in the model is defined as a customer's overall evaluation of the purchase and consumption experience with a product, service, or provider.[3] This definition is quite different from transaction-specific definitions of satisfaction that capture a customer's immediate reaction to a particular episode or experience. Why discard the immediate response in favor of a more cumulative or overall definition of satisfaction? Although it seems more remote, the latter turns out to be more directly tied to customers' repurchase intentions and behavior. Customers' repurchase decisions are affected by their entire purchase and consumption history with a company or brand, not just the last trip to the restaurant or last shipment from a supplier. Although Figure 3.1 lists loyalty, broadly defined, as the desired outcome of satisfaction, there are other constructs we could have shown there as well. Customer satisfaction may also lead to an enhanced reputation and greater brand equity for the company, which will in turn attract additional customers who are disposed to develop loyalty of their own.

The figure also shows overall satisfaction and loyalty in circles, treating them as abstract constructs that can be measured in concrete terms. Overall satisfaction is reflected in different concrete satisfaction measures, which might include a satisfaction scale, how the product or service performs overall versus customer expectations, performance versus an ideal product or service in the category, and performance versus "best in class" competitors. Similarly, loyalty may be measured using a variety of behavioral intentions (ratings of the likelihood that customers will return, will purchase other products and services from the company, or will speak positively of their experience to others) or actual behaviors (such as whether customers do return, how often they return and how much they purchase when they do, and whether they bring or refer additional customers).

Note the dotted arrow that runs from an attribute-benefit cluster directly to customer loyalty in Figure 3.1. This captures the possibility that customers' intentions or decisions to repurchase are affected directly by certain benefits. In a recent study of satisfaction with hair care providers, for example, we found that the quality of the haircut, the relationship with the stylist, and the atmosphere of the salon all affect loyalty via overall satisfaction. However, the timeliness and ease of scheduling an appointment have direct effects on loyalty in addition to their effects on satisfaction. Price can also affect loyalty directly—customers are likely to weigh price or value much more when evaluating loyalty than when evaluating satisfaction. ("I love his work, but I can't afford to go back every month. . . . ")

Developing the Benefits and Attributes Side of the Lens

You can't develop the lens of the customer by sitting around and reflecting on how customers view the world. Instead, you need in-depth, qualitative research to show you the issues from the customers' own perspective. Keep in mind that the goal of conducting qualitative research (such as interviews and focus groups) is not to immediately set priorities for quality improvement—it is to identify a comprehensive range of issues (benefits and attributes) that potentially drive satisfaction, loyalty, and profitability. The customer sample that you use at this stage of the research should represent a good cross-section or range of customers from the population or target market of interest, but it need not be truly random as you're not looking for statistical validity at this point. The lens or model that results from this qualitative research provides the foundation for more systematic survey research, which in turn becomes the primary basis for setting priorities when you get to that stage of the process.

Marketing books offer a wide choice of qualitative methods that you can use to identify product and service attributes and the customer benefits they provide—one-on-one interviews, group interviews or focus groups, protocol methods (having customers "think out loud" while using or evaluating a product or service), and a variety of observation techniques.[4] Here, we focus on one qualitative technique that is particularly well suited to the development of a customer model or lens: the *critical incident technique* (CIT).

The CIT can be used to identify satisfaction drivers for a range of internal and external customers. It typically involves an interview in which individuals or groups of customers are asked to provide a list of the things that they like and dislike about the product, service, or company in question. According to Bob Hayes, an expert on the CIT approach, "A critical incident is a specific example of the service or product that describes either *positive* or *negative* performance. A positive example is a characteristic of the service or product that the customer would like to see every time he or she receives that service or product. A negative example is a characteristic of the service or product that would make the customer question the quality of the company."[5]

The critical incidents themselves should be as specific as possible in describing a single feature of the customer's purchase and consumption experience. Hayes argues that a good critical incident should cover a single behavior or characteristic, and should either describe the service provider in behavioral terms or describe the service or product using specific adjectives. Consider two examples from the case study in Appendix A, which describes CIT interviews with tire retailers. One retailer noted positively that "the range (variety) of products is good"—pointing to a particular characteristic of the tires (the available range) using a specific adjective (good). Another retailer noted negatively that "regional representatives arrive too seldom"—pointing to a specific behavior of the local salesperson (waiting too long between visits).

If the critical incidents are too general, the interviewer needs to ask additional questions to clarify what the customer really has in mind. For each specific incident, it is also useful to ask the customer for comments on the significance and consequences of the incident. Such questions will elicit valuable information for the next stage of the process, categorizing the incidents into attributes and benefit groupings. When encouraged to elaborate, for example, the retailer who praised the product range pointed out that carrying a range of tire products allowed him to offer "a tire for almost every customer that walks into my store." The one who said the regional representative arrived too seldom said that "he should come every month . . . just to see how things are going."

Steps in the CIT Process
Overall, the CIT process involves a number of steps that are helpful to describe using an activity-based flowchart. Figure 3.2 illustrates the flow of the CIT research process.

Step 1 is to compile and assess whatever relevant secondary research or knowledge pertaining to the lens of the customer already exists within the company. (One should avoid, of course, any biases from the lens of the organization.) Perhaps similar studies have been conducted in slightly different research contexts that shed light on how customers view the product or service.

Step 2 is to make initial visits to different customers early in the process. We have found this important for two reasons. First, the visits will provide firsthand observations of the

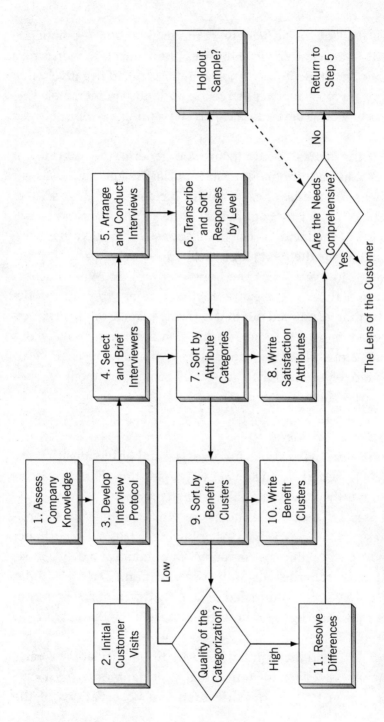

Figure 3.2. Process Flowchart for CIT Research

customers' world. Imai refers to this as visiting *gemba*, a Japanese word that means the "real place" where a product or service is produced, purchased, or consumed.[6] Observing what goes on in the context of the purchase or consumption experience provides an understanding of attributes and benefits that may not arise in the context of an interview or focus group. Kano refers to these as *basic* or expected attributes.[7] Examples of these basic attributes include a car that should always start or food products that should always be clean. A second purpose of the customer visits is to gain an understanding of the way customers are likely to react to the research and the methods to be used. Essentially, it provides an opportunity to pretest and fine-tune the CIT interview process.

Step 1 and Step 2 provide the information you will need for Step 3, where you develop an interview protocol. The protocol is a plan that can be given to the CIT interviewers as basic instructions for conducting the research. It includes directions on how to start, conduct, and finish the interview. It also includes lessons that can be passed along from the initial customer visits and company knowledge. For example, just how many likes or dislikes should the interviewers ask the customer to provide?

A sample interview protocol for the tire study is provided in Section 1 of Appendix A at the end of the book. In the initial customer visits and pretests, we learned that customers were much more forthcoming with dislikes than with likes. We thus instructed the interviewers to ask customers for a range of five to ten likes as well as dislikes, but we emphasized that if the customer had trouble coming up with five likes, the interviewer should move along to the dislikes. The protocol contains instructions to ask respondents to be more specific when they are too general. Once the critical incidents are specific, the interviewers are instructed to ask customers for the benefits and consequences of the incidents by asking, "Why is that important to you?" or "How does that affect you?"

Step 4 is the process of selecting and training interviewers to use the protocol, in those cases where the primary research team is not conducting all of the CIT interviews. If the team is doing its own interviewing, the step can be compressed to a brief discussion to assure that everyone shares the same understanding of the interview and its purpose.

Step 5 is the process of formally arranging places and times to conduct the interviews with a sample of customers and then completing the actual CIT interviews. Hayes recommends conducting between ten and twenty customer interviews for a given customer segment or grouping. This is only a starting point; the number may increase depending on the rest of the analysis.

In Step 6, the written or taped comments are formally transcribed or organized to separate the critical incidents from the customers' comments regarding their consequences. These transcriptions comprise the raw output of the CIT interviews. Section 2 of Appendix A contains a sample output of CIT interviews.

The next four steps encompass the coding of the critical incident data into attributes and benefits by judges working independent of each other. Before proceeding to these steps, however, it is advantageous to create a holdout sample. This sample should include anywhere from 10 percent to 20 percent of the customer interview transcripts selected randomly from the overall sample of interviews prior to their analysis. This holdout sample will be used after Step 11 to assess the comprehensiveness of the attributes and benefits.

The beauty of the critical incident technique is that it taps into customer perceptions using specific customer memories that are salient and relatively easy for customers to retrieve. Yet these positive and negative incidents are not satisfaction attributes per se. Rather, the incidents reflect some specific level of an attribute on which customers' experiences vary. Thus the first step in the coding procedure (Step 7 in the overall process) is to have

independent judges sort the critical incidents into their underlying attributes. Recall that an attribute, in this context, describes
the more concrete aspects of the product or service (such as size,
speed, price, and so on).

Returning for the moment to the convenience store example, say that one customer comments positively on the abun-
dance of parking spaces at her local outlet and how fast the
checkout people are. A different customer may, in contrast, comment negatively on the scarcity of parking spaces at his outlet
and how slow the checkout people are. The researcher's job is
to identify that both customers are referring to the same two
concrete attributes, the availability of parking and the speed and
efficiency of the checkout staff, on which they receive very different levels of performance. Figure 3.3 illustrates the process of
coding the critical incidents into shared concrete attributes. In
Step 8, the researcher writes out a list of the coded satisfaction
attributes. These satisfaction attributes should be stated as neu-
trally as possible (availability of parking, speed and efficiency
of employees) so as not to bias respondents when the attributes
are rated in a subsequent survey.

Once the critical incidents are coded into attributes, the attributes are then coded into a set of benefit categories. The researcher makes a personal judgment as to what the customer is
referring to and uses information obtained in the follow-up questions to sort the attributes. The goal is to sort the attributes into
benefits that describe the more general or abstract qualities that
customers derive from the attributes. If you are familiar with
quality control techniques, you will notice that this process is
similar to using affinity diagrams to group quality attributes into
higher-level categories. If the groupings are unclear, it is useful
to ask customers themselves to perform the sorting process.

Consider again the convenience store example. When asked
about the significance of certain attributes, customers respond
that four attributes (availability of parking, speed and efficiency

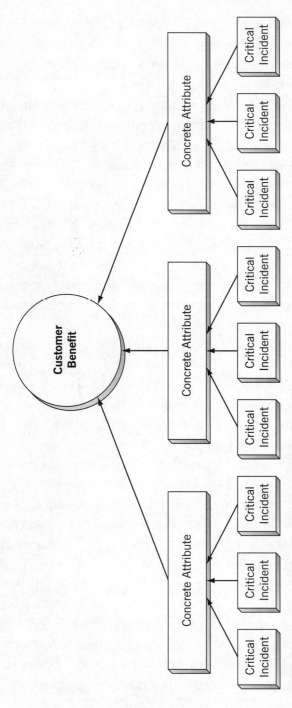

Figure 3.3. Coding Critical Incidents into Attributes and Benefits

Source: Adapted from Bob E. Hayes, *Measuring Customer Satisfaction: Survey Design, Use, and Statistical Analysis Methods,* Milwaukee, WI: ASQ Quality Press, 1998, p. 21.

of employees, hours of operation, and location) all share the common benefit of allowing them to get in and out of the store with what they need when they need it. The attributes are all central to providing the convenience benefit that is central to a convenience store. Once the researcher (or customer) sorts the various attributes into benefit categories, the benefit clusters are formally written out in Step 10 of the process.

One must then stop to assess the reliability of the attribute and benefit categories. The purpose is to evaluate the quality of the judges' categorizations. The inter-judge agreement, or *reliability*, is the percentage of critical incidents that any two judges group into the same attribute category, and the percentage of attributes they group by the same benefit. The percentage ranges from 0 (all items are grouped differently) to 100 percent (all items are grouped exactly the same). Hayes suggests an agreement index of 80 percent as a reasonable cutoff to determine whether the groupings are reliable, which is consistent with our own experience.[8]

Following Figure 3.2, if the reliability of the categorization is high, any differences among the judges are resolved in Step 11. The research team discusses the differences in their various categorizations and resolves the differences by mutual agreement. The end result is a common coding of attribute and benefit categories across the judges. If the quality of the categorization is low, the process returns to Step 7 and the research team discusses why the quality of the categorization is so poor. The team may decide to have a new independent judge (or customer) perform the sorting and coding process to determine if one of the initial judges was either not clear on the task or performed the task poorly. The team may even determine that the interview notes do not provide enough information for the judges to perform their task properly and that the judges need more data.

Once the quality of the categorization is high and the differences among the judges have been resolved, the judges should conduct a final evaluation to determine the comprehensiveness of the lens. The holdout sample, which contains interviews that were transcribed but never shown to the judges who coded the data, reenters the process. Each judge studies the holdout sample to determine whether it contains attribute or benefit information not already included in the coding. If there is nothing new in the holdout sample, the range of customer needs captured in the attribute and benefit categories is judged comprehensive. The result is an initial customer model or lens that provides a basis for subsequent survey development and data analysis. If, however, customers in the holdout sample raise a significant number of new issues, the needs may not be comprehensive and more customer interviews should be conducted. This returns the CIT process to Step 5 (arranging and conducting interviews) and a new coding or updated coding process is performed.

Tables 3.1 and 3.2 present examples of comprehensive customer needs from an analysis of qualitative data for convenience stores and cell phones, respectively. The examples show the difference between the concrete aspects that describe the convenience stores and cell phones and the benefits they provide.

In cell phones, the battery duration and reception quality are concrete attributes that contribute to product functionality as a benefit. The tables also highlight why it is critical to obtain this information from the customers' perspective. Notice, for example, that service quality for convenience stores does not include the speed and efficiency of the employee. As mentioned earlier, customers view this particular employee-based attribute as more central to convenience than to service quality. In the cell phone example, it is interesting that customers distinguish between the basic functionality of the cell phone and what they perceive to be more innovative or distinctive features (high-tech features such as e-mail capabilities and the availability of digital technology).

Table 3.1. **Attributes and Benefit Categories for Convenience Stores**

Benefit Category	Satisfaction Attributes
Quality of service	▪ Accuracy of the checkout ▪ Friendliness of the employees ▪ Attentiveness of the employees ▪ Grooming and appearance of the employees
Product offerings	▪ Stock or availability of products ▪ Brand names of products ▪ Variety and selection of products ▪ Freshness of the coffee ▪ Freshness of the non-coffee products
Store layout	▪ Ability to find what you need ▪ Neatness and orderliness of displays ▪ Feeling or sense of fun you get when walking through the store
Prices	▪ Overall value ▪ Competitiveness of gasoline prices ▪ Competitiveness of store prices ▪ Frequency of sale items
Cleanliness	▪ Cleanliness inside the store ▪ Cleanliness outside the store ▪ Cleanliness of the rest rooms
Convenience	▪ Convenience of the location ▪ Hours of operation ▪ Speed and efficiency of employees ▪ Availability of parking
Safety	▪ Lighting of the premises ▪ Ability to see what is happening in the store ▪ Feeling of safety and security
Motorist services	▪ Accuracy of signs, gauges, and meters at the gas pumps ▪ Ability to pay at the pump ▪ Availability of car wash ▪ Availability of air and water for vehicles ▪ Working operation of equipment such as gas pumps and air
Separate takeout food	▪ Accuracy of food preparation ▪ Quality of takeout food

Table 3.2. **Attributes and Benefit Categories for Cellular Phones**

Benefit Category	Satisfaction Attributes
Cell phone design	▪ Size ▪ Weight ▪ Appearance ▪ Accessories ▪ Color covers ▪ Uniqueness of design
Product functionality	▪ Battery duration ▪ Reception quality ▪ Ease of use ▪ Reliability ▪ Ability to find replacement parts
Innovation	▪ Common features (such as memory and tones) ▪ High tech features (such as e-mail and organizer features) ▪ Product portfolio ▪ Availability of digital technology ▪ Availability of Analog technology
Prices	▪ Overall value (prices paid for quality received) ▪ Competitiveness of prices versus other brands ▪ Bundled offers (phone plus network service)
Quality of service	▪ Network support ▪ Repair service ▪ Replacement plans ▪ Customer service plan
Branding	▪ Brand of cellular phone ▪ Brand of network service ▪ Phone model

You will better understand the value of CIT data when building the lens of the customer after you have completed the exercise in Section 2 of Appendix A. The Appendix includes the raw output of several CIT interviews conducted with independent tire retailers who are direct customers of a tire manufacturer. Your task is to use the critical incidents and the information in the probing questions and comments to identify satisfaction attributes and to group the satisfaction attributes into benefit categories using the blank CIT analysis worksheet.

It is important to note that the usefulness of the qualitative interviews does not end with the construction of an attribute and benefit lens. As the case in the appendix illustrates, the interviews contain a wealth of customer-based ideas for product and service improvement that often turn out to be quite valuable once quality improvement priorities have been set.

Developing the Satisfaction and Loyalty Side of the Lens

The analysis thus far provides details of the front end of the lens of the customer model depicted in Figure 3.1. As described earlier, the attributes provide customers with benefits and the benefits drive overall satisfaction. To complete the lens, you need to add any desired consequences of satisfaction that you want to include. For this chapter, we'll limit consideration to those consequences requiring customer assessment or evaluation in a survey. The addition of consequences that require data from other sources (such as company records of actual customer retention or profit per customer) is taken up in Chapter Five.

Customer loyalty is perhaps the most important and natural desired outcome of satisfaction to be modeled in the lens and included in any subsequent customer survey. As this loyalty shows itself in a variety of ways, companies often collect multiple loyalty measures in the survey and use them to create a loyalty index. The choice of particular loyalty measures for a given company and customer segment is a matter of customizing the construct and measures to fit the immediate circumstances. If your company sells directly to an end user, the loyalty measures that interest you most may be customers' intent to repurchase the product when they need a replacement and to recommend the product to friends and family. If you are an industrial supplier, it may be more important to know whether or not satisfaction will increase your account penetration and your customers' propensity to push the product along to an end user.

Figure 3.4 illustrates a lens of the customer model that combines benefits, customer satisfaction, and the consequences of interest for the convenience store industry. The benefit categories (from Table 3.1) are shown as potential drivers of satisfaction with a convenience store. (The attributes that combine to produce the various benefits are listed in the table.) The lens shows how customer loyalty is a direct outcome of satisfaction in the model.

Should Reputation Have a Role?

We suggest that you view reputation as an outcome rather than a driver of satisfaction.[9] Collecting the satisfaction and reputation measures simultaneously in a survey means that the reputation evaluations are colored by customers' recent purchase and consumption experiences. In addition to this confounding effect, reputation acts as a type of overall evaluation, making it problematic as a driver of satisfaction, which is itself an overall attitude or evaluation.

In the past, reputation has been modeled as a psychological anchor that affects perceptions of quality performance as well as satisfaction. This is certainly appropriate if you measure the customers' perceptions of reputation prior to the purchase and consumption experience and then subsequently compare the results with measurements in a quality and satisfaction survey—it

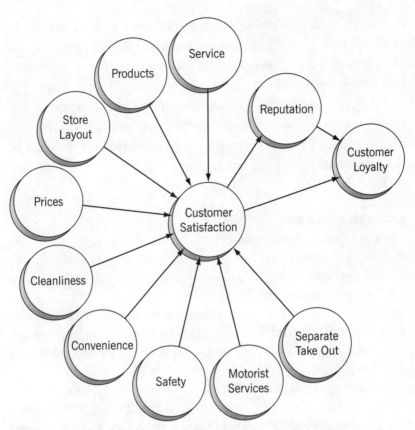

Figure 3.4. A Quality-Satisfaction-Loyalty Model for Convenience Stores

is only the attempt to compress the measurement into a single step that poses problems.

As shown in Figure 3.4, satisfaction is modeled as having direct effects on both loyalty and reputation. The effect of satisfaction on loyalty is the degree to which customers' more recent purchase and consumption experiences affect loyalty.

The effect of satisfaction on reputation reflects both the degree to which customers' more recent purchase and consumption experiences enhance a product's or service provider's reputation and the consistency of customers' experiences over time. Finally, reputation may have a direct effect on loyalty by way of such factors as the ongoing inclusion of certain brands in a customer's *consideration set*—the brands the customer looks at before making a choice—and more long-term or memory-based evaluations of the brand.

Loyalty in the convenience store model is thus viewed as a function of both the ongoing reputation of the store and the customer's satisfaction with more recent performance. Results of this model are presented in Chapter Five.

CHAPTER SUMMARY

The lens of the customer provides the central focus for your customer measurement system. This lens should accurately reflect the range of attributes and benefits that matter to your customers in their purchase and consumption experiences. This may not be the same as the lens of the organization, or how your company views the products and services it provides. Qualitative research is essential to building the lens of the customer. It provides you with a template for subsequent survey development and data analysis.

A particularly valuable qualitative technique used at this stage of the research is the CIT approach or critical incident technique. The approach has customers list specific things they like and dislike about their interactions with your company and its products and services. When combined with questions designed to elicit customers' views of the implications or consequences of the incidents, the approach generates a wealth of interview data that can be used to build the lens of the customer.

As with many information management systems, the development of effective customer measurement and management is a process where the maxim "garbage in, garbage out" really applies. Unless you take the time and effort to properly conduct qualitative research and thoroughly understand the nature of customer perceptions, all subsequent stages of the process are compromised. A poor customer lens will result in a customer survey that does not contain the language and attribute-benefit structure your customers perceive. It will also cause problems later on when you statistically analyze customer data.

In contrast, a well-developed lens provides a blueprint for both survey development and data analysis. It provides a model around which different functions within your organization can build consensus. Rather than a representation of what the engineers or marketers in the company think, it is a reflection of what your customers think. Completing the lens requires a thorough understanding of just what you expect from a satisfied customer, whether a repeat purchase, an increased sales volume in related areas, or a recommendation to a prospective new customer. In the next chapter, you will see how to use a completed lens to develop and administer a quality-satisfaction-loyalty survey.

Questions for Consideration

1. How much of your company's customer research is dedicated to qualitative methods such as observations, one-on-one interviews, or focus groups?
2. What role does qualitative research play in your customer measurement and management process? How is it analyzed, and how is it used?
3. What is *loyalty* for your customers? In other words, what do you hope to gain by increasing quality and customer satisfaction?

Building the Quality-Satisfaction-Loyalty Survey

You'll usually need several sources of data to establish all the links from quality through to profits. Consider the experience at Sears and Volvo. Sears uses one survey to measure internal quality in the form of employee perceptions and attitudes and a second survey to measure external quality and satisfaction from the customers' perspective. Information from both sources is then combined with financial performance information for individual stores to trace the links in the employee-customer-profit chain.[1] Volvo tracks internal quality with engineering-based measures of vehicle performance, and uses customer surveys to track external quality.[2]

In this chapter we focus on ways to develop and administer the survey that measures customer perceptions of quality, satisfaction, and loyalty. The lens of the customer—built from the qualitative research in Chapter Three—will serve as a blueprint for your survey, identifying the attributes to include and the order they should appear. To make the survey results useful, however, you will also need to specify and include measures of satisfaction and loyalty so as to be able to combine the individual customer responses into a meaningful pattern of causes and effects.

■ Step 1: The Preliminaries

As in any other activity, if you don't know what you want to get out of customer measurement, it's going to be hard to tell if you've found it. So before you develop the survey itself, you need to figure out what information is required—which is a function of what you're planning to do with it—as well as how to segment your customer base, what survey method or methods to use, and how to sample the population.

What Information Is Required?

Start by restating in simple terms what you want your customer survey to tell you, and what you plan to do about it. This might be as generic as "We want to know what our customers want so we can give them more of it—and what they don't want, so we can avoid including it," or it might be tailored to your particular business. Then look back at the lens of the customer and list the attributes and benefits it identifies as having the potential to drive customer satisfaction and loyalty.

Then list some direct questions about customer satisfaction and loyalty. From a statistical standpoint, these are the primary dependent variables that the model is to explain based on customer perceptions of attribute and benefit performance.

Make sure that the things you're asking about are at least partially under your control, so the results will be meaningful and useful. There is no point in finding out that your customers are uniformly unhappy that every day they get a day older, unless you're in the business of providing some way to preserve youth and prolong life. So consider just how the results will affect areas and individuals in your organization and what actions you may need to take based on the results.

How to Segment Survey Respondents?

The next step is to figure out which market segments to include in the survey—and just how to classify respondents into those segments. The choice of segments should be based on their importance in your strategic market plans. Beyond the choice of key segments (such as "daily" and "weekly" convenience store customers), another important question related to segmentation and sampling is whether to include current, past, or potential customers in the research. Companies are often content to focus only on current customers. Unfortunately, if current customers are systematically different from those you've lost or those you would like to pursue in the future, your results from a current-customer survey could be misleading or incomplete.

Market segment classifications may be based on information collected prior to the survey. Existing research may already have determined which customers are classified into which segments. If survey respondents can be identified and classified into segments beforehand, then it is perhaps unnecessary to have segment-related information in the survey itself. Otherwise it will be critical to include information in the survey that allows you to sort or select customers by segment. The sorting or selection criteria may be direct or indirect.

The Indirect Approach

Using the indirect approach, you might include descriptive items in the survey such as demographic variables (age, sex, income level, education level, ethnic background), geographic variables (city, country, or geographic area), and experience-related variables (frequency of purchase or consumption of the product or service, confidence in evaluating the product or service, and so on). These measures would then be analyzed *after* the surveys are administered to develop distinct clusters or groups of customers that differ on the variables of interest (such as male versus female or frequent versus infrequent convenience store customers).

This approach is indirect in the sense that the descriptive measures are only proxies for identifying more needs-based segments (see Chapter Two). A disadvantage of this approach is that it can lead to the inclusion of so many descriptive variables that the survey becomes long and cumbersome. An advantage of the approach is that it provides a database that can be used to develop and identify new segments. This allows you to *cut,* or sort the data, in various anticipated and unanticipated ways. Descriptive variables are typically collected near the end of the survey. If a customer feels sensitive about answering particular questions (such as age, income, or education level), encountering such questions up front may bias the responses to the whole questionnaire or lead the customer to give up on it entirely.

The Direct Approach

Using the direct approach, you provide an existing segmentation within which customers place themselves in a needs-based segment. Often companies have some existing knowledge of the major segments or populations in their customer base. If simple descriptions of each of the different segments can be included in the survey, customers can indicate directly which segment they most identify with. For the convenience store survey, for example, independent research conducted prior to the survey helped us define five major segment profiles. We then used the profiles to develop descriptive statements for each segment:

Segment 1: I tend to visit a convenience store several times a day for snacks as well as meals.

Segment 2: I am a parent who occasionally goes to a convenience store mainly to buy fill-in items, emergency items, or things for the kids.

Segment 3: I visit a convenience store daily to buy one or two items such as a soda, coffee, cigarettes, or candy.

Segment 4: I go to a convenience store once or twice a week to buy a snack, soda, or coffee.

Segment 5: I shop at a convenience store less than once a week, mainly to buy snacks and party items or items for a trip.

In the resulting convenience store survey (presented in Appendix B at the end of the book), we asked survey respondents to indicate which of these statements best described their behavior. The primary advantage of this approach is that it is based directly on an existing segmentation scheme. This greatly simplifies the analysis of the survey data. The responses are simply sorted according to their segment identification and analyzed. The disadvantage of using existing segment profiles is that it assumes that the profiles provide an accurate description of the underlying segments. If the nature of the segments changes between the segmentation study and the quality-satisfaction-loyalty survey, the results of the latter will be skewed in unpredictable ways.

We recommend using a hybrid of the direct and indirect segmentation approaches when possible. Using existing segment profiles simplifies subsequent analysis and bases the analysis squarely on a segmentation scheme. But it is helpful to include some additional descriptive questions. The convenience store questionnaire, for example, augments the segment-level questions with a small number of demographic questions used in U.S. census questionnaires. The hybrid approach allows for some exploratory analysis using the demographic variables to sort or cluster respondents into new segments. The demographics also provide descriptive details of the segment profiles, such as whether "daily" convenience store customers tend to be male, female, older, younger, and so on.

What Survey Methods to Use?

Prior to developing the survey, you also need to decide just how to communicate with customers and administer the survey. The choice of survey methods has important implications for the nature of the questions and scales involved. There are various approaches, the more common being one-on-one interview surveys, telephone surveys, Web-based surveys, and written surveys. Each method has its strengths and weaknesses. The choice of methods should depend on the context.

One-on-one interviews are well suited to business-to-business applications, where the population of customers is relatively well defined (such as those customers who purchase a certain type of chemical or part). Conducting personal interviews is a good way to increase response rates; it shows customers that you are deeply interested in their opinions. This is important if your organization has a reasonably small number of key customers that you want to take special care of. A disadvantage of one-on-one interviews is that they can become difficult to manage when the sample of respondents is large. Problems also arise when the individual conducting a survey interview has a vested interest in the results of the survey, as when the salespeople's bonus system is tied to the data that they collect from customers. Anyone who has purchased or leased a new automobile in the last few years might remember the pleas from salespeople to "give me 10s on the survey—my bonus depends on it!" It is crucial to maintain independence and objectivity in these cases through the use of a third party within the company (such as a manager or a salesperson who does not serve that customer) or an independent data collection agency to conduct the actual interviews.

Telephone surveys, particularly those using a computer-aided telephone interview or CATI system, are particularly well suited to end-user products and services where representative samples of consumers are needed from a large population. The convenience store survey script in Appendix B is taken from a CATI application. The advantages of telephone interviews include their relatively low cost per completed interview and the control the interviewer has over who is responding to the survey (compared, for example, to written or mail surveys). A human interviewer can clarify any misunderstandings or problems that a respondent may have in answering a survey question. And when they encounter respondents who are simply not able or willing to respond to the survey, trained interviewers can quickly say thank you and terminate the interview. The disadvantage of the telephone interview approach is that interviewers may generate unpredictable effects of their own. They must be carefully trained, as the way questions are stated is likely to have an impact on how customers respond.

Through the use of randomization techniques (such as random-digit dialing), telephone interviewing typically yields more representative samples of customers in a population than you get with other methods. Using this approach, time zones and area codes can be systematically sampled. The American Customer Satisfaction Index survey, a large national survey, uses this approach to obtain valid cross-sections of U.S. consumers.[3] The survey samples are checked against census data using demographic profiles to ensure that they are properly balanced with respect to age, sex, income and education levels, and ethnic background.

Internet-based surveys are growing in importance as the population of Web users becomes more representative of specific customer groups. Web surveys offer significant advantages in that data can be collected, transferred, and updated continuously online. And unlike CATI survey participants, Web respondents have a written version of the survey available on the computer screen to help keep the questions and scales clearly in mind—and they all see exactly the same questions, which eliminates the danger of interviewer bias. Web surveys have already become the preferred method of data collection in those industries where Web samples are representative of the customer base (as for certain financial services and online retail operations).

Yet many customer populations continue to contain large percentages of individuals from lower income and education categories that do not have direct access to the Web (such as convenience store and mass merchandise retailer customers). This situation is likely to change in the near future. Infrastructure changes, such as the diffusion of broadband cable, will broaden the population of Web users in the years to come. Even now, creative solutions can be used to give more customers Web access for the purpose of conducting a survey. For example, a kiosk system can be placed in a location that all customers could access (such as a convenience store or an employee lounge). A cross-section of customers could be encouraged to use the kiosk using personal communication or incentives (such as store coupons). Easy-to-read touch-screen displays can be used to collect, transfer, and even analyze the data on-line. Another alternative is to use printed versions of the survey that can be handed out or mailed to customers and later scanned and processed on-line.

Written surveys, particularly mail surveys, remain a popular approach to data collection. An advantage of written surveys is their relative low cost *per targeted respondent,* or survey sent. Written surveys can be mailed or distributed efficiently to a relatively large number of customers. The problem is that response rates tend to be low for this approach. Because of the low yield, direct mail often proves more expensive than telephone or Web-based surveys and the respondents are not as representative of the customer population. The quality of the survey data also suffers in that, compared to phone or interview surveys, written surveys offer less control over the interview itself. Written surveys may be passed along for others (subordinates or other family members) to fill out and there is no easy way to clear up misunderstandings or ensure that the respondent is responding carefully to the questions.

One solution to the weaknesses inherent in any one method of data collection is to combine elements of more than one approach. For example, one-on-one or small group interviews can be used to explain the purpose of the survey and motivate participation. To ensure anonymity, written surveys could then be left with the respondents to fill out and return after the interview. Another successful approach in retail contexts is to use store intercepts in combination with written, telephone, or Web surveys. The store intercepts are used to explain the survey and motivate participants to participate in it, while the follow-up survey (in writing, by phone, or by Web page) allows respondents to participate at their convenience.

How to Sample the Population?

Sampling is the process of selecting respondents or customers from a population for inclusion in the survey. Naturally, then, sampling starts with the customer population or populations of interest. Your market segmentation scheme and the specific segments that you have decided to include in the research largely define your customer population. The wide variety of techniques for sampling from customer populations fall into three general categories:

1. Census samples
2. Judgment samples
3. Statistical samples

Census samples involve gathering information from every possible member of a population, such as all of an organization's customers—or all customers in a given segment. Census samples are perfectly representative because the sample and the population are one and the same. Census samples are feasible primarily when the population size is relatively small (such as potential purchasers of jumbo jet engines or highly specialized industrial tools). If you define your population as all customers who have recently recorded transactions, your own records can supply a census sample of current customers.

When the population of customers is too large for a census sample, judgment or statistical samples are called for. Judgment samples involve—as you would expect—using your judgment to decide who should and should not be included. One common method of judgment sampling is to take a list customers and pick people well dispersed with respect to age, sex, income, education, and so on. The drawback is that the inclusion of respondents in the sample is at the discretion of the researcher. This makes it difficult to generalize any results to the population at large. At the same time, this approach is useful when the goal is simply to identify potentially important issues, as when conducting qualitative research. Recall, for example, that the primary goal of using the CIT (critical incident technique) method (from Chapter Three) is to find out what attributes and benefits to include in a more systematic survey.

Statistical sampling involves using statistical probability to determine a sample. Hayes tells us that the primary differences between judgment and statistical sampling are that statistical sampling involves the use of random selection to include cases or respondents in the sample, the ability to statistically determine an appropriate sample size, and the ability to determine how representative the sample is of the population.[4] Thus statistical sampling allows for greater generalization of the study results to the population as a whole. Examples of statistical sampling methods include random-digit dialing of customers (as through CATI systems) and systematic sampling from a customer list (start at a random point and then pick customers at set intervals, say, every tenth or hundredth name, until you have the number you need for your sample). Respondents in the ACSI survey, for example, are selected using random-digit dialing. Naturally, the choice of a sampling method or methods is a function of both the size and accessibility of the customer population or populations of interest and the purpose of the research.

■ Step 1 Continued: Measuring the Performance and Importance of Attributes and Benefits

Once you've cleared away the preliminary survey questions, the next issue that you face in developing the survey is just how to measure benefit and attribute performance and importance. With respect to performance, the survey results should provide reliable and sensitive measures of customer benefits, customer satisfaction, and loyalty. When measuring importance, you must choose between direct customer measures of importance (using, for example, scales or other rating tasks) and derived importance or impact measures based on statistical analysis.

Performance Measures

There are two important factors to consider when you measure perceived customer benefits, customer satisfaction, and loyalty. First is the abstract nature of the constructs involved. Recall from Chapter Three that customers do not obtain satisfaction directly from the concrete attributes and features that describe product and service offerings. Rather, satisfaction and loyalty are a function of the benefits and consequences that the attributes provide. These benefits (such as convenience, safety, and service quality), being abstract or latent constructs, cannot be observed or measured directly using single survey items and scales. The same is true for such overall evaluations as customer satisfaction and loyalty. Abstract or latent variables are reflected in a variety of concrete measures. Benefits are reflected in the attribute ratings that make up the benefit, satisfaction is reflected in a variety of overall performance ratings, and loyalty in a variety of behavioral intentions.

The best way to empirically measure these latent variables is to use multiple concrete *proxies,* or survey measures. For example, qualitative research shows that a convenience store customer's perception of convenience is reflected in ratings of store location, hours of operation, speed and efficiency of employees, and the availability of parking. A latent variable can be measured using a weighted average or *index* of these survey measures. The convenience index of a convenience store thus becomes a weighted average of a customer's ratings of store location, hours of operation, speed and efficiency of employees, and the availability of parking. Overall satisfaction becomes a weighted average of a customer's ratings on such measures as satisfaction, overall performance versus expectations, and overall performance versus a "best in class" competitor.

The second factor to consider when measuring perceived customer benefits, customer satisfaction, and loyalty is the distribution of the data as it relates to your need for *sensitive measures*—measures that can differentiate among fairly small differences in the underlying conditions. This is an ongoing problem in customer surveys because perceptions of quality and satisfaction almost never fall on a normal distribution. That is, there are typically no bell-shaped curves in the data. In a competitive economy, only those competitors with relatively high quality and satisfaction ratings tend to survive. As shown in Figure 4.1, this results in quality and satisfaction data that is strongly *skewed* (where most of the responses are bunched near the high end of

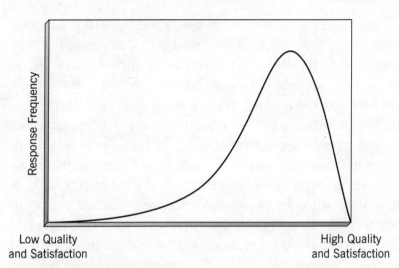

Figure 4.1. The Skewed Distribution of Quality and Satisfaction Data

Low Quality
and Satisfaction

High Quality
and Satisfaction

the quality and satisfaction scale and the tail of the distribution trails off toward the low end of the scale).

The measurement challenge is to be able to distinguish among customers that are crowded together at the high end of the scale. To illustrate the problem, consider what happens if you use a very insensitive measure of satisfaction. When asked yes-or-no questions (say, Are you satisfied?), the overwhelming majority of customers answer yes. In a recent study of airline passengers we found 95 percent of customers responding yes when asked to evaluate their satisfaction on a yes-no scale.[5] Unfortunately, yes-or-no questions give you no way to distinguish among customers that range from moderately to very satisfied. The sensitivity of the scale improves when you move to a 5-point scale (where 1 = poor performance or very dissatisfied and 5 = excellent performance or very satisfied). Research on quality and satisfaction scales suggests that using a 10-point scale is better still.[6] Going beyond 10-point scales, however, is not beneficial as respondents have trouble using all the scale points.

Most sensitive of all is the use of multiple 10-point scale questions to form an index. Consider that any given survey measure is composed of two sources of variation, that which is supposed to be measured (what statisticians call the "true score") and that which is not meant to be measured (the "error"). The *true score* is what the various items in an index have in common, while the *error* is more a function of the biases or problems inherent in individual survey questions. By averaging the measures into a single index, you can increase the amount of true score and reduce the overall error variance (relative to an individual survey measure or question) as error from the individual questions is canceled out. As a result, in statistical analysis and modeling, when you use indices in place of single item measures, you explain more of the variation in satisfaction and loyalty, and the relationships involving quality, satisfaction, and loyalty are stronger. In state-of-the-art quality and satisfaction modeling, the use of indexing to measure abstract or latent variables has become the norm.

Consider a simple example of the value that indices bring to an analysis. When you assess the financial health of your company, you know that any one marketing, accounting, or finance measure (customer retention, return on investment, return on capital employed, stock price) is an imperfect reflection of overall state of the company. Taken together, however, the measures provide a more accurate picture of financial health than is possible using any single measure.

Direct Importance Measures

The next step is to decide whether to use direct or derived measures of attribute and benefit importance. Many satisfaction measurement systems rely heavily on the "gap" model, in which the measure of what needs improvement in quality or satisfaction is the difference between customers' direct ratings of attribute importance and direct ratings of performance (performance minus importance).[7] There are three kinds of direct measures commonly used in marketing research:[8]

1. *Direct scale ratings:* Respondents rate the importance of a product or service's attributes on a scale ranging, for example, from "not at all important" to "very important."
2. *Point allocation methods:* Respondents distribute importance "points" (say 100 points) among a given set of attributes where the proportion of points allocated to an attribute indicates its importance.
3. *Paired comparison ratings:* Respondents rate the relative importance of attribute pairs.

Paired comparison ratings can place tremendous burdens on respondents because of the number of attribute pairs involved. They have also been heavily criticized for producing arbitrary measures of importance.[9]

Direct scale ratings are considered more accurate (less biased[10]) than point allocations and easier for respondents to provide than either point allocations or paired comparison ratings. These factors make direct scale ratings the more popular choice, so the remainder of this discussion will focus on this method of assessing customer responses.

The primary advantage of direct importance scale ratings and the gap model is their ease of implementation. They require minimal analysis (plotting averages and taking difference scores) and can be easily understood at various levels in an organization, from front-line service personnel to CEOs. Yet there are several problems associated with using direct measures. The method assumes that customers understand what you mean by "important" and also that they know just what attributes are important to them—and are willing to tell you about it. In the end, we find that asking customers directly to rate the impact that an attribute has on their satisfaction and loyalty is an extremely difficult task. Direct importance measures often result in socially acceptable or status quo answers and poor discrimination. Using direct scale ratings, for example, respondents have a difficult time differentiating among those attributes that are most important to them. We have rarely found significant differences in importance among the top-rated fifteen to twenty attributes in a survey. Research also shows that the importance measures or weights that people report and those that they use when making a decision often differ dramatically.[11] The insight that direct ratings provide drops off as the number of attributes increases.[12]

We illustrate both the strengths and weaknesses of the gap model using a study in which we examined the drivers of satisfaction for a pharmacy. Approximately a hundred customers evaluated twenty-nine attributes of a retail pharmacy. Figure 4.2 presents the results. The mean values of rated attribute importance are ordered from least to most important and plotted question by question (where 1 = not at all important and 10 = very important). The corresponding attribute performance measures are also plotted (where 1 = poor performance and 10 = excellent performance). The key attributes to improve are those where the "gap" (performance minus importance) is lowest.

On the positive side, gap models are relatively easy to implement, analyze, and explain. The analysis simply involves plotting the two dimensions, importance and performance, and examining their differences. This often makes gap models a good option for companies that are just beginning to develop a customer orientation. The models identify the "low-hanging fruit"—the obvious gaps that need to be closed—and get the company into the habit of monitoring customers. The priority-setting logic is also the same as for the strategic satisfaction matrix (Figure 1.5, described in Chapter One). Attributes on which both importance and performance are rated high are core com-

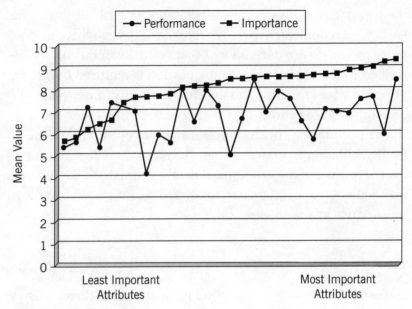

Figure 4.2. **Gap Model Results**

petencies, while attributes with high importance and low performance need improvement.

However, a major problem with the approach is that customers rate most everything as important. In Figure 4.2, twenty-four of the twenty-nine attributes are rated quite high on importance. The conclusion is that the company needs to improve most of the items with low performance ratings, and it's hard to tell which ones would make the most difference to results. Basically, importance scales are effective at highlighting the *least* important attributes but ineffective at highlighting the *most* important attributes. The direct importance ratings are simply not diagnostic. It is primarily the *performance* measures that drive the priority-setting process.

Another problem with direct importance measures and the gap model is that the survey has a tendency to grow. Because the approach requires at least two ratings for each attribute, the survey becomes nearly twice as long as a survey where importance measures are derived by other (statistical) means, as described in the next section. One question is required to rate an attribute's performance and another to rate its importance. Direct importance ratings may be the only option when the customer population (or the sample size) is too small or ease of implementation is an overriding concern. Where feasible, however, it is much more economical to take the statistical approach and add good dependent variables, such as satisfaction and loyalty, for use in a regression analysis.

Derived Importance Measures

Importance measures do not need to be measured directly. They can be derived statistically from attribute performance ratings and ratings of overall satisfaction. Because statistical estimations are more objective and less biased, they are often superior to direct customer ratings.[13] Statistical analysis provides estimates of importance as the impact that one variable has on another. Customers indicate how they perceive a product or service to perform on a number of attributes as well as their overall satisfaction and loyalty. Variation in performance and satisfaction across customers allows the researcher to estimate (using regression or regression-based statistical techniques) the impact that different aspects of quality and value have on satisfaction and loyalty. Statistically determined importance ratings can avoid many of the problems that you encounter with direct importance ratings.

But the quality of the statistical estimates can vary significantly. *The important question is whether or not the estimation builds on the lens of the customer!* The lens should be viewed as a blueprint for both survey development *and* analysis. A major problem facing regression-based estimates of impact or importance centers on the correlation among the drivers of satisfaction. If attribute ratings are too highly correlated, that is, if changes in one rating tend to follow changes in another without regard to outside factors—what statisticians refer to as lacking sufficient *independence*—the statistical estimates of impact may be poor.

The lens of the customer, which is based on thorough analysis of qualitative research, shows just which attributes go together in the customer's mind. By combining multiple attribute ratings together into benefit indices, the lens provides a means of reducing correlation among the satisfaction drivers; it increases their independence. The result is a set of benefit and attribute importance weights that are superior to those that can be collected directly from customers.

■ Developing and Administering the Survey

Once you go through the background analysis outlined thus far, you'll be in a position to develop a survey instrument you can use with confidence. The process described here follows the flowchart presented in Figure 4.3, which we have found useful in developing and administering our own quality-satisfaction-loyalty surveys. The first part of this chapter covered Step 1 (the preliminary decisions regarding what information to collect and how to collect it), so the discussion here starts with Step 2 and goes through the rest of the process. Appendix B at the back of the book provides a sample output in the form of a finished survey script from the National Association of Convenience Stores (NACS). We refer to this survey throughout the process to illustrate our recommendations.

Step 2: Develop Opening Statements

The primary purpose of the opening statement is to persuade your targeted respondents to take part in the survey. There are

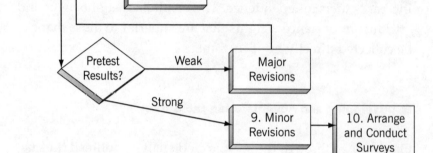

Figure 4.3. Flowchart for the Quality-Satisfaction-Loyalty Survey

three main messages that can be communicated in an opening statement to help maximize the response rate:[14]

1. Emphasize the importance of the topic or problem area to respondents.
2. Emphasize that the primary purpose of the research is to better understand the problem.
3. Emphasize that the organization or entity conducting the research will use the results to improve the situation.

In the convenience store survey, the emphasis in the opening statements is on the latter two points. The statements point out that the survey is meant to understand what quality areas are important to convenience store customers and that the results will be used to guide quality improvement efforts.

The opening statements may also include screener questions needed to identify customers. The convenience store survey screens respondents to include those individuals who have visited a convenience store within the last three months. The screener in the survey also provides an explanation that convenience stores do not include grocery store chains, drug or discount stores, or mass merchandisers. If asked, the interviewer explicitly defines a convenience store as "typically a small franchised market that is open long hours." These explanations and definitions were added as a result of pretesting and revising the survey.

Step 3: Explain the Scales

Once respondents have been screened and agree to participate, their first task is to evaluate attribute performance levels. In some cases the ratings may only apply to the product, service, or retailer of interest (say, stores in the Seven-Eleven chain). In other cases the ratings may apply to multiple competitors (say, Seven-Eleven, Quik Stop, and other widely known chains). Before providing the information, the survey must instruct respondents on how to perform the task. This includes who or what is being rated and how to use the scales.

The types of scales and their explanation depend partly on the method used to collect the data. If, for example, it is important to explain multiple anchors on the scale (such as what a 1, 2, 3, 4, or 5 actually means in the context of the survey), it is easier to do this in a written or Web-based survey where respondents can refer to the written anchors. It is more difficult to do so in a telephone survey. Because the respondent has no written list to refer to, the emphasis is typically on keeping only the two endpoints in mind. In the convenience store survey, for example, it is explained that a rating of 1 means poor performance and a rating of 10 means excellent performance.

Keep in mind that the choice of scales and the need to label scale points depends on the researcher's approach to measurement. Given the abstract nature of the constructs and the need for sensitive measures, we strongly advocate using indices to measure customer benefits, customer satisfaction, and loyalty. The use of indices gets you away from very concrete, individual scales where each point on the scale is ascribed some meaning. Indices resemble temperature scales—they just show that the reported value is higher or lower than some benchmark. The meaning you attach to the index levels is based on how a product or service performs against competitors and over time. By deemphasizing concrete scale points in favor of more sensitive indices, you have less need to ascribe meaning to anything more than the end points. We recommend using 10-point scales, where 1 is poor and 10 is excellent, to evaluate performance across data collection methods.

Step 4: Arrange Attribute Questions by Benefit Category

The next sections of the survey present all of the attributes the lens of the customer research recommended for evaluation. The lens of the customer provides a blueprint as to how the attributes are organized—how they go together in a customer's mind. The survey should leverage this lens and present the attributes in clusters defined by the benefit categories (quality of the service, product offerings, store layout, and so on). Particular to the convenience store survey is the inclusion of two questions at the beginning of this section to assess customer perceptions of store reputation. As described in Chapter Three, these ratings will be used in combination with overall satisfaction to explain customer loyalty.

Step 5: Develop the Satisfaction Questions

Satisfaction is the customer's overall evaluation of his or her experiences with a product or service provider. In your subsequent analysis, it will be a major dependent variable that you will explain using your measures of attribute and benefit performance. Satisfaction is a latent variable that will be manifested in a variety of more concrete performance ratings. As we have said, it is critical to combine multiple measures of satisfaction in a satisfaction index. In addition to a simple rating of satisfaction, other measures include evaluations of overall product or service performance against different benchmarks. You might ask customers to evaluate performance versus their expectations, versus an ideal product or service provider in the category, or versus a "best in class" competitor.

Notice that we do not advocate using any one of these as a proxy for satisfaction. Rather, satisfaction as a latent or abstract construct is what all of the various evaluations have in common. The measures simply represent different benchmarks that customers use to evaluate performance and from which an index can be constructed. The convenience store survey has respondents evaluate performance using three different questions. The first asks them to express overall satisfaction, the second asks for an evaluation of performance versus expectations, and the third seeks an evaluation of performance versus an ideal product or service in the category. These questions were modeled directly on those used in the ACSI survey, which have been shown to provide a very reliable and sensitive measure of satisfaction.[15] An added benefit of using the ACSI questions is that it allowed us to benchmark the survey results for convenience stores against other industries and firms included in the ACSI survey.

Step 6: Customize the Loyalty Measures

Whereas satisfaction measures apply more or less universally across industries and contexts, loyalty measures do not. As discussed in Chapter Three, the desired outcomes of satisfaction are highly specific to the nature of the business, product, and service involved. Volvo, for example, has specified a range of desired customer outcomes, from the repeat purchase of a Volvo vehicle to the purchase of Volvo financing, Volvo insurance, the purchase and use of a Volvo gas card, and the spread of positive word-of-mouth advertising. If your customers are retailers who turn around and sell your product to end users, loyalty may take the form of the *push*—the sales effort they make on your behalf—as in the "Råtorp Tire Company" case in Appendix A. If your product is a once-in-a-lifetime purchase (a piece of jewelry or a collector's item), loyalty may involve the customer's willingness to buy other products or services from you (cross-selling) and to tell other potential customers about your offerings. In an industrial context, the level of satisfaction may have little effect on whether a customer buys at least some of your products and services. At the same time, it may have a great effect on just how *much* they buy (account penetration). Another desired outcome may include the trust that customers place in you and their resulting commitment to maintaining a relationship.

Our point is simply that, whereas satisfaction measures are more or less universal, loyalty measures must be customized. In the convenience store survey, the desired outcomes for the store chains and franchisees are rather straightforward. They include enhancing the customers' likelihood of visiting the store again in the future and their likelihood of recommending the store to others. The measures used in the Råtorp Tire Company survey were quite different. As in the convenience store survey, they included the likelihood that the customer (in this case a retailer) would continue to purchase, but they also included whether the proportion of products ordered from the manufacturer would likely increase or decrease in the future (account penetration) and the degree to which the retailer would recommend the manufacturer's products to its customers (push).

Step 7: Add Descriptive (Segmentation) Questions

Descriptive questions (including market segment profiles and demographic questions) are typically added near the end of the survey. As noted earlier, the main reason for this placement is that the questions, being more personal in nature, are apt to lead a respondent to terminate the survey if asked early on. Once the interviewer has developed some rapport with the respondent and the interview has the momentum provided by answering the performance, satisfaction, and loyalty questions, descriptive information is often easier to get.

The primary purpose of the descriptive questions is to group customers by characteristics such as age and income level for later analysis, so as to track their representativeness and discover possible new segments. Recall that the convenience store survey contains both a direct question regarding segmentation and a group of indirect demographic questions that can be used to segment or describe customers. The direct question presents the five segment-defining statements listed toward the beginning of this chapter and asks respondents to select the one statement that best describes their use of the convenience store. As noted earlier, the primary benefit of having respondents self-select into preexisting segments is the ease of subsequent analysis. The drawback is that it presumes that the segments do not change or evolve significantly over time.

Steps 8 and 9: Pretest and Revise the Survey

A golden rule of survey research is to conduct one or more tests before you put any survey into the field. The primary purpose of preliminary testing is to identify and resolve whatever problems respondents might have in answering the questions. Pretesting tells you whether the survey is able to collect the desired information, and where you need to reword questions to make them simpler and easier to understand. In Figure 4.3, a strong pretest (few problems encountered) leads to minor revisions prior to arranging and conducting the surveys. If the pretest is weak and major revisions are required, the revised survey should be tested again before being put into the field.

Pretesting is not just the domain of those who administer the survey; it can raise questions of strategic relevance to top management as well. Another rule we like to follow is to involve both those directly involved in the survey process and those who will use the information to make resource allocation decisions. In pretesting the convenience store survey, for example, we learned several lessons. One was that many people were unclear as to just what a convenience store was in the first place. Does it include gas stations that sell some other merchandise? Grocery store chains that sell gasoline? This led to the inclusion of more specific screening questions and definitions that the interviewer could use as needed.

Pretesting also raised questions about what benchmarks the customer should use to evaluate the competitiveness of a convenience store's prices. Should the benchmarks be limited to other convenience stores, or should they include other stores that sell similar merchandise (such as grocery stores for bread, milk, and soft drinks). Based on top management input, it was decided to let customers compare prices to other stores at which they may buy similar merchandise. The reason was that executives at the various chains were very interested in the gap between perceived and actual price differences between convenience stores and other types of stores. Whereas convenience stores are often perceived as having relatively high prices, actual price differences are often small or nonexistent.

Step 10: Arrange and Conduct the Survey

Just how the survey is arranged and conducted is largely a function of the method of contact. Telephone surveys often involve random-digit dialing or random selection from a customer list. The interviewer makes a pitch for participation and, if the time is not convenient, can arrange for a better time to call back. Before collecting survey data in a one-on-one interview, the respondent is usually called and an explicit appointment is made. Recall that store intercepts are also a valuable tool for selling the survey—persuading people to take part in later administration either by phone, Web, or mail. Web surveys may use an e-mail message to introduce and gain interest in the survey and then instruct the respondent on how to access the survey. Customers may also self-select to participate in surveys that are available on a company's Web site.

Just who administers the survey is a function of both the sheer number of respondents and the need for objectivity. We suggest that people within the sponsoring company administer the survey themselves as long as the number of respondents is not too large and administrators can remain objective. As argued in Chapter One, a truly customer-oriented company should not routinely leave the job of collecting customer data to outsiders. But for a large-sample survey, it will be more cost-effective to use a professional data collection firm. If the interviewer's compensation is a function of customer responses (the number of "10s" on the survey), the objectivity of the responses and resulting data will be compromised. If a more objective interviewer cannot be found within the company, it would again be best to use a third party to collect the data.

CHAPTER SUMMARY

The development of a quality-satisfaction-loyalty survey builds directly on the lens of the customer. Survey development should not be a process in which people from different parts of a company sit around and decide what *they* would like to see on the survey. Rather, the lens of the customer provides a blueprint for deciding which attributes to include and the benefit categories to use for organizing them. Even before developing a survey it is important to understand what populations or market segments to survey, what data collection method or methods to use, and how to sample from the target populations.

In leveraging the lens of the customer, the construction of a quality-satisfaction-loyalty survey should follow certain guidelines. Benefits, satisfaction, and loyalty are abstract constructs that cannot be measured directly using any one concrete survey item. They are best measured using an index of multiple measures or proxies. Indices also provide for more sensitive measures than single survey items, so they can explain more of the variation in satisfaction and loyalty and are better at identifying important satisfaction drivers.

The importance that customers place on attributes and benefits has traditionally been determined by two different approaches: direct measures of importance and those derived from statistical analysis. Among the different direct measures, direct scales (ratings from "not important" to "very important") are often preferred. They are straightforward to collect and as good as or better than other direct approaches (such as point allocation or paired comparisons). Yet, when done properly, statistically derived measures of importance are better than direct measures at objectively capturing the impact attributes and benefits have on satisfaction and loyalty. It is important for statistical analyses to leverage the lens of the customer when grouping variables for analysis. Otherwise, even the most rigorous statistical estimates may be a poor reflection of reality.

With the lens of the customer in mind and the data collection methods chosen, you can complete the survey instrument in a systematic way. First, assess attribute performance by benefit category. After that, obtain overall evaluations of satisfaction. Then select loyalty measures and customize them to fit the product, service, or context. To some, loyalty is simply a matter of whether a customer comes back to buy the same product or use the same service. To others, loyalty is a matter of how much more customers will buy (account penetration) or what else they will buy (cross-selling). After adding descriptive questions to help identify market segments, pretest the survey to identify any unforeseen problems. Arranging and conducting the survey yields the data that serves as input to the next phase of the process. In Chapter Five we focus on using this data to derive the information needed to set priorities and improve product and service quality.

Questions for Consideration

1. Obtain a copy of the main satisfaction survey that your company sends to customers. What are the overall strengths and weaknesses of the survey?
2. Does your company rely on direct importance measures, statistically derived importance measures, or both when setting quality improvement priorities? What are the strengths and weaknesses of your approach?
3. Are there any steps in the flowchart for survey development (Figure 4.3) that you choose to skip? If so, what effects might this have on the quality of your customer survey and resulting data?

From Data to Information

Analyzing Quality, Satisfaction, Loyalty, and Profit Data

When it comes to analyzing your customer survey data, you have a lot of options. We recommend a variation on *principal-components regression (PCR)* that is relatively simple to use and provides as much detailed information as you need to make quality improvement decisions. It combines two statistical methods: principal-components analysis and regression analysis. *Principal-components analysis* is a data reduction tool that shows what any group of survey measures have in common, so you can develop the benefit, satisfaction, and loyalty indices. *Regression analysis* relates these indices to each other and lets you determine the benefit, satisfaction, and loyalty impact scores.

As in earlier chapters, we present a flowchart to illustrate the necessary steps used to apply PCR to the lens of the customer. To support our recommendation, in Appendix C at the end of the book we compare results achieved using this method against the results of other approaches.

We begin by describing just what information you can and should be obtaining from your analysis. After describing our data analysis method, we end the chapter with a discussion of how to link survey data to financial performance measures, illustrating the links with examples from Volvo and a major hotel chain. These financial links, which highlight the payoff from investments suggested by customer measurement, will help you inspire people to make real quality improvements based on the information the survey process develops.

■ The Required Outputs of a Measurement System

When you analyze satisfaction and loyalty data, you're really looking for answers to two relatively simple questions. Where does your company need to improve quality or value to increase satisfaction and loyalty? And once satisfaction and loyalty are improved, what are the payoffs? These questions follow directly from the framework we presented in Chapter One, a simplified version of which appears in Figure 5.1. The basic assumptions are that improved quality leads to increased satisfaction, which in turn makes customers more loyal, and that you get more profit from loyal customers than from those who don't care where they get the product or service you're selling.

Now, how do you quantify the links? The prerequisite is that your measurement system should provide sensitive *and* reliable measures. Your goal is to provide managers with truly diagnostic information—with levers they can push to improve quality and satisfaction. You don't want results that suggest that

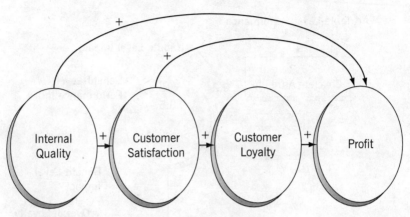

Figure 5.1. The Logic of Customer Satisfaction Modeling

everything (or nothing) is important, or results that show differences (as among competitors) or changes (over time) that are not valid and meaningful. In other words, you want a system that produces results you can trust. Finally, you want to be able to predict what happens when satisfaction increases. How likely are customers to come back and how much more revenue or profit will they generate?

To make your measurement system a reality, you will need to analyze your survey data to produce multiple levels of information in the system. These different levels are illustrated in Figure 5.2. The circles in the figure labeled "satisfaction" and "loyalty" are the key to understanding your customers' overall consumption experience. Best measured using indices made up of multiple concrete measures, these abstract constructs are important in benchmarking performance versus competitors and tracking performance over time.

The customer benefits in Figure 5.2 are also indices, or weighted means, calculated from the values of the concrete attributes of your products and services that provide the benefits. These benefit-level indices are the heart of the lens of the

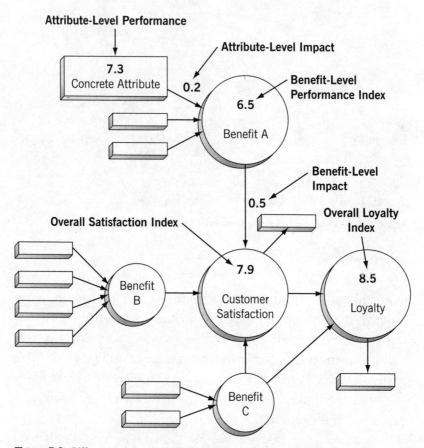

Figure 5.2. Different Levels of Information in a Satisfaction Model

customer. They provide an overall view of how you are performing in quality areas as defined by your customers. But because these indices are abstract, they cannot be acted upon directly. Action requires moving down to the level of the underlying concrete attributes.

Attribute values are obtained directly from the quality-satisfaction-loyalty survey ratings. They are represented by the rectangles in Figure 5.2. The figure shows sample performance information at each of the different levels, the satisfaction and loyalty indices, a benefit index, and one of the attributes of the benefit. Each is measured using a 10-point scale like the ones in the convenience store questionnaire in Appendix B. For the benefits and attributes, 1 is poor performance and 10 is excellent performance.

But setting priorities requires you to measure impact as well, that is, the extent to which a change in an attribute will lead to a change in satisfaction, loyalty, and other desired customer outcomes. As there are attribute and benefit levels of performance, so there are also attribute and benefit levels of impact. The benefit-level impacts (obtained from the regression analysis described later in this chapter), indicate how much impact each benefit has on customer satisfaction. It is helpful to focus initially on these benefit-level impacts to gain an understanding of the consumption experience. Looking at the attribute or question-level impacts (obtained from the principal-components analysis also described in this chapter) will help you relate your improvement efforts to the everyday activities of the company that have the highest payoff. Attribute impacts are more the focus of continuous improvement efforts, while benefit impacts are the focus of innovation efforts—attempts to find completely new ways to deliver the benefits that customers value. The impact information in Figure 5.2 shows an attribute-level impact of 0.2. This shows that a 1-unit change in the attribute or question is associated with a 0.2-unit change in the benefit index. A benefit-level impact of 0.5 shows that a 1-unit change in that benefit index is associated with a 0.5-unit increase in the satisfaction index.

Once you have impact information at every level of the model, you can quantify the change that improving an attribute or benefit would make in loyalty (and subsequent profitability, once this data is added to the model). The impact of changing an input to the model (an attribute) on the output of the model (loyalty or profitability) is simply the product of all impacts in the chain of causes and effects. (Where there is more than one path or chain of cause-and-effect relationships, it would be the sum of the different impact chains.)

■ Introducing PCR and an Alternative

If you are familiar with traditional PCR,[1] you will see that our approach to principal-components regression has some unique features. Traditional PCR factor-analyzes all the attribute ratings simultaneously to produce a set of independent components or factors. It ignores benefit clusters of the type we recommend you develop using qualitative research to create the lens of the customer. The problem is that the approach is too data driven; the factor analysis dictates the lens. In contrast, our approach uses the benefit groupings or clusters in the lens as a theory or model to structure the PCR analysis. This approach provides the technical sophistication and diagnostic information that your analysis requires.

The main alternative to using our version of PCR is *partial least squares* (PLS). Both our PCR approach and PLS use the lens of the customer as a guide to structure the analysis. PCR is a two-step approach in which the benefit, satisfaction, and loyalty indices are first estimated using a series of principal-components analyses. The researcher then uses these indices or latent variables in a series of regression models to estimate a causal chain of events (as from quality through to financial performance). PLS performs both of these steps for the researcher. It estimates an entire causal chain or model using an iterative estimation procedure that integrates aspects of principal-components analysis and multiple regression. Researchers in the areas of quality, marketing, and consumer research regard PLS as the state of the art in customer satisfaction modeling.[2]

The disadvantage of PLS is that it requires special software and training, and the software is neither user-friendly nor easy to find.[3] If you have mastered PLS, by all means use it. At a conceptual level, our flowchart and procedure for evaluating the quality of your analysis still applies. Otherwise, we recommend that you use PCR, which is straightforward to do using easily available and user-friendly software packages. In Appendix C we demonstrate just how similar the results are with PCR and PLS. Comparing the two approaches we find a 0.99 correlation in estimated benefit-level impacts and a 0.98 correlation in estimated attribute-level impacts. In other words, the results are virtually identical. The following sections describe how to analyze a customer satisfaction model using our PCR method.

■ Analyzing Data with PCR

The sole purpose of analysis is to make sense out of the data you collect. This section includes a step-by-step guide to analyzing data sets that you can use if you're in charge of performing or managing the data analysis (see Figure 5.3). Even if you're remote from the actual research and your responsibility is to create an environment where customer data will be developed and used, the guide will still be useful as it will demystify the process and, as a consequence, make you more constructively critical when evaluating the output of an analysis.

Notice the overall pattern of the flowchart in relation to Figure 5.2. The first major accomplishment will be to create the latent variables for benefits, satisfaction, and loyalty. Then the process will go on to derive the actual values for the impact of one level of the model on the next, and to establish benchmark values for the benefit, satisfaction, and loyalty indices. The combination of impacts and indices will provide the cause-effect chain.

To illustrate the process and the different results, we use a data set that was collected using the National Association of Convenience Stores (NACS) questionnaire described in Chapter Four. The data includes computer-aided telephone interview results from a national sample of 1,024 U.S. convenience store customers. For simplicity, the figures given here reflect the entire

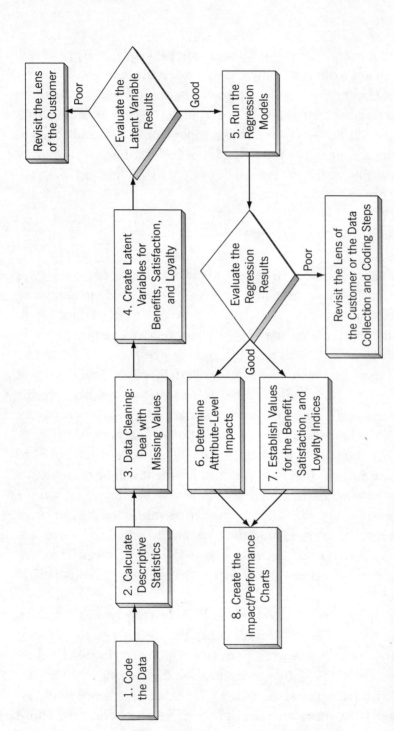

Figure 5.3. Flowchart for the Steps of Data Analysis

population of users rather than the detail for the segments that we identified.[4]

The satisfaction model used as a basis for the questionnaire is reproduced in Figure 5.4. We have assigned a number to each benefit in the figure. That number corresponds to the numbering of the questions in the survey that relate to the benefit (see Appendix B). For example, questions 2.1 through 2.4 in the survey are all service-related questions under the benefit labeled "2 Service."

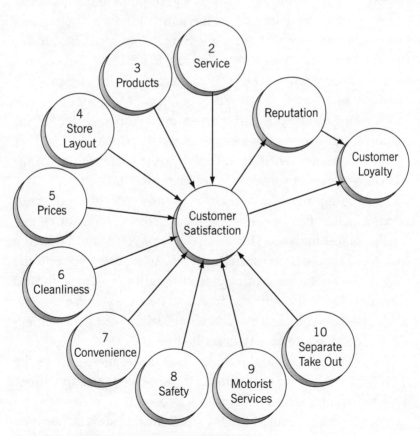

Figure 5.4. The NACS Convenience Store Model

Step 1: Code the Data

Prior to conducting any analysis, you must code the questionnaire results into a computer data file. *Coding* means creating and consistently applying rules for transferring information from one format (a questionnaire) to another (an Excel worksheet or a file for a statistics package such as SPSS). Basically this means that numbers are assigned to each of the answers. Customer satisfaction questionnaires usually have interval scales—the 5-point or 10-point scales that make for easy coding.

There are two main types of "missing" values. In one type, respondents have simply chosen not to respond to the question. In the other type, respondents have indicated a response in a "do not know" category for a given question. It can be fruitful to code these two differently to be able to separate the answers later on. For instance, use (–99) as the code for missing values and (–88) as the code for the "do not know" category.

Coding can be difficult if questions are open-ended. If, for instance, questions such as type of work, education level, or market segment identification ask the respondent to come up with a free-form answer, the researcher must take the time and effort to categorize and sort the responses. Deciding on categories ahead of time and offering them to the respondent greatly facilitates the analysis. This is, again, why you should take the time to do qualitative research and build the survey around the lens of the customer. Your up-front qualitative work should serve not only to identify attributes and benefits but also to show you what customers are like and what variable categories or levels you need to adequately describe them.

Once the data is in the computer files, be sure to check the quality of the coding and editing of the survey questionnaires. This needn't be complex or exhaustive—just look over the responses for each question for any irregularities, such as response codes that were not available on the survey or response patterns that are too repetitive, suggesting that respondents were not thinking carefully about each question. Numbering the questionnaires makes it possible to go back and correct any errors.

Step 2: Calculate Descriptive Statistics

Now that you have the data in an electronic medium, the real analysis starts. The first step is to get to know the data. You can learn a lot by using simple tools such as frequency tables, scatter plots, cross tabs, mean values, and standard deviations. *Frequency tables* simply describe how frequently respondents use the different values on the survey scales. They help you to understand the percentage of missing values and whether there is sufficient variation in your data.

Too many missing values are a signal that respondents had a difficult time responding to your question. It may be because they did not understand the question or have no experience with the attribute in question. For example, in the NACS survey there are questions concerning motorist services and separate take-out food. Yet not all convenience stores sell gas or have a separate take-out food service.

You need to have variation before you can carry out any type of multivariate analysis. Frequencies are an initial check that you at least have some distribution in the responses. *Cross tabs* are used to study frequencies of two variables in one table to determine if they are related. Again this is a necessary first check of your data to determine whether the questionnaire has worked as planned.

Step 3: Deal with Missing Values

Generally, statistical analyses such as multivariate regression ignore customers for whom data is missing on any one variable in the analysis. The consequence is that an entire customer's data is ignored because one data point (the answer to one question) is missing. As a result, you should fill in or provide estimates for the missing data before analyzing the data set. The easiest and most common approach is *mean value substitution,* which replaces the missing values for a variable with the mean value of that variable based on all valid responses. That is, if a customer fails to provide a response when rating the "availability of parking" for convenience stores, the mean of those customers that do respond is calculated and inserted for the missing value.

Although common, mean value substitution creates other problems and should be used with caution. The approach assumes that customers who provide answers are the same as customers who do not, an assumption that should be tested before replacing the data. There a number of ways to do this.[5] The easiest way is to divide the data into those with and those without missing values on a variable. Then you test whether there are significant differences between the two groups on other variables. A simple and useful technique to do this is *one-way ANOVA* (analysis of variance) in which missing versus nonmissing is used as a factor (0/1 variable) and mean values of all the other variables are compared.

When the percentage of missing values is small (less than 5–10 percent), mean value substitution does not create great problems and is a simple solution. As the percentage increases, there are other ways to salvage variables. Most statistics packages (SPSS, SAS, Systat) offer several ways of replacing missing data such as the use of means, medians, nearby points, linear interpolation, or linear trends. But as mean value substitution is widely used, you must be aware of its four main disadvantages:[6]

1. Imputing the mean assumes that cases are missing completely at random—and thus only randomly different from nonmissing cases. Unfortunately, missing variables on such variables as income or education level are unlikely to be at random.

2. The approach fails to use information on other variables that may improve the accuracy of the imputations, such as the fact that income and education are generally related.

3. The distribution of responses produced by the method is distorted—spiked at the mean where all the imputed cases are located. A consequence is that variance on the measure is underestimated (by approximately the percentage of sample cases with missing data). Standard errors for regression coefficients and other statistics become biased as well.

4. Because the imputed values are a constant and therefore unrelated to other variables of interest, correlations with these other variables are reduced and estimated regression coefficients (impact scores) biased.

Step 4: Create Latent Variables for Benefits, Satisfaction, and Loyalty

Up until now we have described a normal procedure to prepare your data for any type of multivariate analysis. The next step is to start creating the latent variables that are built into the questionnaire. As described in Chapter Four, a *latent variable* is an abstract measure or construct that you measure using multiple concrete proxies or subdimensions. At this step of the process, what you produce are standardized variables or indices for use in your regression models. These standardized variables have a mean of 0 and a standard deviation of 1. Later, under Step 7, you will translate these standardized variables into more meaningful performance benchmarks (such as the original 1 = poor to 10 = excellent performance scale).

The way you create the latent variables is to run as many principal-components analyses as there are latent variables in your model. As described earlier, principal-components analysis is a data reduction tool that determines how much variation the analyzed variables have in common. In the convenience store model, you would first analyze the four measures for service (questions 2.1 through 2.4), then the five measures for products (questions 3.1 through 3.5), and so on. Your interest is only in the first component in each analysis. (The *first component* shows just what the set of measures has most in common—that is, what they principally or primarily capture.) As a consequence you should restrain the statistical software to save only the first component or factor (as a variable in the data set) when extracting the principal components.

In this description we assume that the researcher has specified a model structure based on the lens of the customer, with multiple questions measuring each latent variable in the model (benefits, satisfaction, loyalty, and so on). This approach is preferable to the alternative of using factor analysis to identify the latent variables across all attributes after the data is collected. In our experience, such data-driven approaches do not capture the lens of the customer as well as you can with up-front qualitative research because customers are more complex than data. They often distinguish, conceptually, among areas of performance that a purely data-driven approach would group together. Customers may also group conceptually coherent areas together that a purely data-driven approach might separate.

In the end, we find that that there is no good substitute for doing thorough qualitative research up front to build the lens of the customer and design a good questionnaire. The work spent up front is rewarded by better results and time saved when analyzing the data. Results from a poorly designed questionnaire are difficult to salvage in later analysis.

How Good Are the Latent Variables?
The following comments will be especially useful if you're already familiar with statistical techniques—and especially if you're the one responsible for conducting the statistical work. But it's a good idea to keep reading in any case, even if this section turns into heavy going, as the material will help you de-

velop a general feel for the process whether or not it proves to be completely clear to you.

The latent variables you develop need to be evaluated prior to using them in a regression analysis. There are two aspects you should look at. First, does each latent variable measure only one aspect of the service, product, or company of interest? Second, does each latent variable measure a different benefit or aspect of the service, product or company?

You can study the Eigenvalues from each principal-components analysis to understand just how good the extracted latent variables are. *Eigenvalues* are measures (provided in the software's output) that capture the variance explained by the factor relative to the total amount of variance in the input measures. If, for example, there are four measures (attributes) in the analysis, and the attributes were completely independent of each other, each attribute would explain 25 percent or one-fourth of the total variation among the attributes. If the attributes are correlated (because they measure the same benefit or construct), a weighted mean or index of the variables should explain more than 25 percent—that is, more than its fair share—of the variation among the measures. An Eigenvalue is simply the variation explained by a principal component divided by its "fair share." When greater than 1, the Eigenvalue exceeds its fair share of variance explained. This suggests that the original measures (such as the attributes of a benefit) can be combined to form a meaningful index (such as the benefit itself). Ideally each principal-component analysis that you run should reveal one large Eigenvalue, which is greater than 1, while the other components (Eigenvalues) extracted are less than 1.[7]

Table 5.1 shows the Eigenvalues for the satisfaction latent variable in the NACS example. The first component has an Eigenvalue of 2.1 while all other components are clearly below 1. From the table we also find that the first component extracted captures 70 percent of the total variation among the attributes. This shows that

Table 5.1. Eigenvalues for the Satisfaction Measures in the NACS Model

Principal Component	Eigenvalue	Percent of Variance Explained	Cumulative Percent of Variance Explained
1	2.10	70.02	70.02
2	0.49	16.42	86.44
3	0.41	13.56	100.00

Extraction Method: Principal-Components Analysis

the three measures provide for a good latent variable or index that captures most of the information in the original measures.

You should then check the correlations among the various latent variables that you will be using as input to the regression models. Ideally, the latent variables that you will use as independent variables at the regression stage in your analysis should be relatively independent. Again, this is unlikely to be the case in customers' perceptions. But using the lens of the customer as a guide should reduce the cross-correlation enough to run the regressions and obtain meaningful impact scores. *Cross-correlation* is simply a term meaning that there are relationships among a whole set of measures. If the correlations are too high (cross-correlation is too severe), it suggests that two benefit indices may be measuring the same underlying benefit and that you need to revisit the coding of your qualitative data and the lens you constructed. Otherwise, as when you simply regress all survey attributes against satisfaction, your results may be illogical or hard to interpret.

We suggest that you explicitly examine the correlations among the various latent variables that you have extracted as a result of the principal-components analyses. After saving the latent variables as new variables in the data set, run a bi-variate correlation analysis among them. When the variables are scaled in the same direction (where higher values indicate higher or better performance), the values should range from 0 (no relationship) to 1 (perfect relationship). Our experience suggests that, for PCR (and PLS) to work well, the correlation between any two benefits should not exceed 0.7, and the lower the values the better. It is especially critical to identify any groups of benefit indices that are highly correlated. In the convenience store data there were only two correlations above 0.6 (out of thirty-six possible), which suggests that the cross-correlation is not too severe.

Step 5: Run the Regression Models

You have now the necessary input to run a series of regression models and identify the critical links in your quality-satisfaction-loyalty model. One of the main purposes of running the regression models is to establish the benefit-level impacts (or beta coefficients). PCR is relatively straightforward to apply if you have access to a statistical software package. (Appendix C also includes a set of instructions for performing PCR using SPSS software.) The beta coefficients obtained from regressing the benefit indices against satisfaction provide the benefit-level impact scores.

Returning to the NACS example, a PCR analysis was carried out using the nine benefits in Figure 5.4 as independent variables and satisfaction as the dependent variable. The resulting R^2 measure (variance explained) for the PCR analysis was 0.618. As seen from Figure 5.5, the benefit with the highest impact on satisfaction is safety, followed by prices and store layout. The benefit with the lowest impact on satisfaction is motorist services. This does not imply that motorist services is unimportant at some level. Rather, it just has little impact. The results show that convenience stores are simply not differentiated on this benefit.

As illustrated back in Figure 5.1, you should also link satisfaction to other variables such as loyalty and profit. When using PCR, you do this by running a series of regression models.

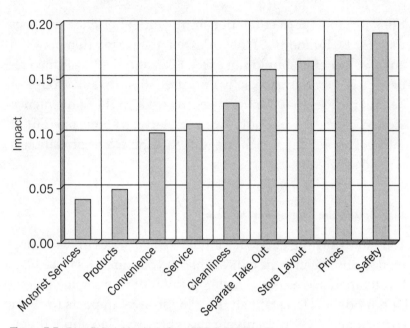

Figure 5.5. Benefit-Level Impacts from PCR Ordered by Size

Figure 5.6 illustrates the different regression models required in a PCR analysis of the convenience store model from Figure 5.4. The latent variables are used as input to three separate regression models (labeled 1, 2, and 3). In the first, the benefits are the independent variables and satisfaction is the dependent variable. Satisfaction then becomes an independent variable in a model where reputation is the dependent variable. Finally, both satisfaction and reputation are independent variables and loyalty is the dependent variable. The series of regression models shows how each part of the model influences customer loyalty.

Evaluate the Regression Results
If your customer lens is sound and you follow the research process described here, troubleshooting at this point should be minimal. A primary indicator of trouble is negative regression co-efficients or impacts in the model (assuming that all the measures

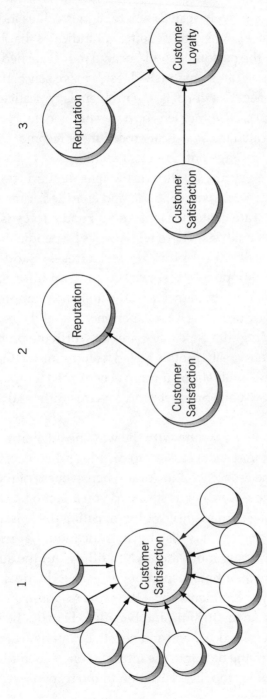

Figure 5.6. Regression Models Used to Estimate the Convenience Store Model

and indices are positively scaled, where higher values indicate better performance). A negative coefficient indicates that if you reduce a benefit the customers will become more satisfied with you, which in most cases obviously doesn't make sense. If your analysis reveals negative impacts, the problem is typically either a poorly developed customer lens or poor survey data. No matter how sophisticated the statistical procedure or technique used, the "garbage in, garbage out" rule still applies.

Needless to say, the quality of the lens depends on how well the qualitative data was collected and analyzed. Time spent building an accurate customer lens and a good survey is time saved during the analysis. There will always be people in your company who will want to tack on measures—to add "just a few" extra questions to the survey to pick up information they're curious about—but any such additions will compromise the lens the survey develops. Our experience is that the benefits gained from adding things post hoc are not worth the problems that these additions create. Simply stated, compromising the lens compromises the analysis. You must accept the fact that customers often view your products and services differently than you do.

If there is nothing wrong with the way the qualitative data was collected, it may be necessary to recode and reanalyze the data. Perhaps the reliability and comprehensiveness of the lens (see Chapter Three) were not as strong as you assumed. Chances are that you will gain new insights by revisiting the lens.

Negative impacts may also be an indication that respondents were not highly motivated when filling out the survey. They should take their time responding to each individual question. If too many respondents circle the same response over and over from attribute to attribute and benefit to benefit, the result will be extreme cross-correlation and negative impacts. There will be no way to turn the data into the information needed to make decisions, as there is too little variation in the responses. As described in Chapter Four, computer-aided telephone interviews help you monitor a respondent's level of motivation during data collection.

Step 6: Determine Attribute-Level Impacts

You now have all the information you need to determine attribute-level impacts and establish benchmark values for your benefit, satisfaction, and loyalty performance indices. The information we use here and in Step 7 involves the benefit and attributes of "safety" from the NACS model, which is presented in Table 5.2. To calculate the attribute impacts, you will need the principal-components analyses run earlier and the standard deviation for each question. In the output of each principal-components analysis you will find attribute-level weights (also known as *factor score coefficients*). These are weights that the statistical software used to construct the standardized principal component that you extracted.

The first step is to divide each of these weights by the standard deviation on the question to produce attribute-level impacts. Since all your principal components were standardized (mean = 0, standard deviation = 1), you cannot use the attribute weights directly as impacts. You have to translate these weights back to their original scales, or undo the standardization, when determining impact. To perform this translation, divide the attribute-level weight by the standard deviation on the question. This results in a more meaningful set of impacts that relate directly to changes in the original scale. Among attributes whose standardized weights are equal, this step effectively emphasizes the impact of an attribute with less variance over the impact of an attribute with more variance.

As seen in Table 5.2, once we divide the attribute weights by their standard deviations, attribute 8.1 (lighting of the premises) has even more impact on safety than the standardized attribute weights (component scores) would suggest.

Table 5.2. Determining Attribute Impact and Establishing Benefit Performance

Survey Item	Benefit/Attribute Label	Attribute Weight	Standard Deviation	Attribute Impact	Attribute Performance	Benefit Performance
	Safety					8.37
8.1	The lighting of the premises	0.26	1.70	0.152	8.57	
8.2	The ability to see inside the store	0.16	1.85	0.086	8.14	
8.3	Your feeling of safety and security	0.23	1.83	0.125	8.30	

Step 7: Establish Values for the
Benefit, Satisfaction, and Loyalty Indices

To establish benchmark values for the benefit, satisfaction, and loyalty indices, you will need the attribute-level impacts calculated in Step 6 and attribute-level performance as expressed by the attribute means. As you saw back in Step 4, an index is calculated using a weighted average of all attributes (questions) included in a latent variable. The idea is to have the attributes that contribute most to the principal component have more weight when establishing the performance levels. Because you are establishing an unstandardized index at this step, one that relates to your original scales, you use the attribute impacts calculated in Step 6 as the weights to establish the benchmark values for the index. The algorithm to do this is quite simple and can be stated as follows:

$$\text{BENEFIT PERFORMANCE INDEX} =$$
$$((i_1 \times a_1) + (i_2 \times a_2) + \ldots (i_n \times a_n))/(i_1 + i_2 + \ldots i_n)$$

Where i_1 through i_n are the attribute-level impacts for attributes 1 through n and a_1 through a_n are performance values for the same attributes. Each performance value is multiplied by its impact, the products are summed, and the sum of the products is divided by the sum of the impacts. The last step transforms the weighted average back to the original scale values for the attributes (1 = poor, 10 = excellent). In Table 5.2, the benefit-level performance for safety is 8.37. Index values for the satisfaction and loyalty indices are calculated in the same fashion, where the multiple measures for the satisfaction or loyalty index replace the attributes in the example.

Step 8: Create the Impact-Performance Charts

Back in the hotel example in Chapter Two (see Figure 2.3), we introduced impact-performance charts to help you understand customer data. Such charts provide a convenient way to represent impact and performance information and serve as a primary input to the development of a strategic satisfaction matrix (see Figure 1.5). The impact of each benefit (or each attribute of a benefit) is plotted against its performance as shown in Figure 5.7 for convenience store safety. The benefit in this case has an impact of 0.2 and a performance level of 8.37. The values are not particularly meaningful until all benefits (attributes) are plotted for comparison (as shown in Figure 5.8). But it helps to understand and emphasize just what the values in the chart mean.

In this case, the impact indicates the effect that a change in the benefit has on satisfaction. An impact of 0.2 means is that if safety increases by one unit (such as one standard deviation for a standardized variable, or one scale value on the 1 = poor to 10 = excellent scale for an unstandardized variable), satisfaction will also increase by 0.2—or 20 percent on its own measurement unit (0.2 of a standard deviation or scale value). The performance level is the degree to which a product or service has achieved a high or low level of performance on the benefit. As described,

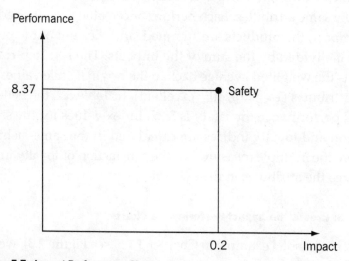

Figure 5.7. Impact-Performance Chart

the performance level is a weighted average or index of performance of the attributes of safety.

Figure 5.8 illustrates the benefit-level impact-performance chart for the NACS model that we constructed using the entire industry sample. In the figure, safety shows up as one of the key competitive advantages (high impact, high performance) for the industry as a whole. In contrast, separate take-out and store layout are aspects that could be improved and have high impact on satisfaction (high impact but lower performance).

Note that "prices" should be viewed quite differently from the other benefits. In most cases, you do not want to improve—that is, cut—prices directly. Unless you want low prices as a core competency, the goal is usually to improve on other benefits to

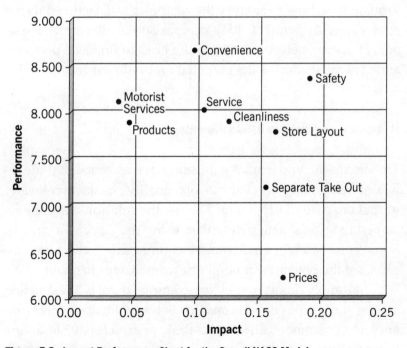

Figure 5.8. Impact-Performance Chart for the Overall NACS Model

take the customers' mind off the price dimensions. In Figure 5.8, prices must be characterized has having low performance and high impact. But the solution may not be to start cutting prices. As emphasized in Chapter Six, your decisions also depend on how your competitors are performing.

Next you would look deeper into your data to determine just what attributes of each benefit you want or need to improve. If, for example, safety is something you want to continue to improve, you should look to the attribute impact and performance information in Table 5.2. The attribute titled "your feeling of safety and security" has a relatively low attribute performance and a relatively high impact, making it a good candidate for improvement.

This ends our discussion of the steps of PCR and the flow diagram in Figure 5.3. Again, if you are interested in more information on how to analyze the customer satisfaction data we refer you to Appendix C for a comparison of alternative methods. However, before examining the links to financial performance, we must address the potential for nonlinear relationships.

■ A Note on Nonlinear Relationships

The discussion and analyses thus far have assumed that the relationships among the elements of a quality-satisfaction-loyalty model are essentially linear. That is, the relationships are assumed to be adequately described using the slope of a straight line. Yet research in quality and customer satisfaction has emphasized the potential for nonlinear relationships in quality data.

In Kano's classic model, for example, there is a distinction among three types of relationships between attribute performance and customer satisfaction.[8] Basic or *expected* attributes are those performance dimensions that customers take for granted. They are presumed to have little impact on satisfaction, unless of course a company fails to provide them—in which case the impact on dissatisfaction is huge. The result is a marginally decreasing (or negative quadratic) effect of performance on satisfaction, where performance has its greatest impact on satisfaction at low levels of performance. What Kano calls "spoken" or *performance* attributes are those on which customers voice their appreciation of continuous improvement. These should have an approximately linear effect on satisfaction. Finally, *surprise and delight* attributes are those that customers do not expect and presumably have a marginally increasing (positive quadratic) effect on satisfaction. These are the "wow" features that really differentiate very high-performing products and services.

Research on the effects of satisfaction on loyalty has also posited and found systematic nonlinearities.[9] When switching barriers are high (when it is difficult for customers to switch from one brand to another), loyalty is affected more at lower levels of satisfaction (a marginally decreasing or negative quadratic relationship). If customers are essentially hostages to a supplier, as with the airline customers mentioned in Chapter Two, they must be quite dissatisfied before they decide to switch. In contrast, when competition is abundant and choices are many, customers must be very satisfied before they stop being mercenaries—that is, give up the benefits of problem-solving or shopping behavior—and become loyalists or apostles of any one brand. The result is often a marginally increasing (or positive quadratic) effect of satisfaction on loyalty. In other words, there is often a rather high "trigger point" on the satisfaction scale where merely satisfied customers are transformed into loyal customers.[10]

On the other hand, we have found that concern over nonlinearities when analyzing quality and satisfaction data is often unwarranted, especially when it comes to attributes and benefits. Although nonlinear relationships certainly exist, they tend to be observed more over time (as surprise and delight attributes become performance attributes, and performance attributes become basic or expected attributes) or across market segments. For any given market segment at one point in time, a linear relationship is all that is usually called for. Indeed, where nonlinearities do occur they suggest that more than one market segment is involved and should have been analyzed separately.

Nonlinearities are more likely for the effects of satisfaction on loyalty and retention. Thus it is wise to explore for possible nonlinearities using scatter plots of the variables in your data set, especially involving satisfaction, loyalty, and other desired customer outcomes. When present, nonlinear relationships can be captured in the regression stage of PCR by, for example, adding quadratic and cubic terms to one or more of the regression models (as between satisfaction and loyalty).

■ Links to Financial Performance

The rest of this chapter illustrates the links from quality and satisfaction to financial performance. Our models thus far have relied on loyalty or customer intentions as a proxy for actual retention and subsequent performance. But intended loyalty is only a proxy. It is no substitute for understanding actual customer behavior and the returns from quality improvement. To estimate the link from quality to behavior, we must address two important issues. At what level of aggregation can your data be linked, such as the level of individual customers versus stores or franchisees? And how and when should you measure the customers' behavior after conducting the quality-satisfaction-loyalty survey?

With regard to the aggregation issue, you need to connect the responses in the questionnaire to some level of desired outcomes, such as actual behavior or financial returns. This requires data beyond the questionnaire, ideally in regard to each customer's behavior and profitability. For example, as part of the analysis of the Volvo data described later in this chapter, we connect individual customer repurchase data and profit per customer with the results of a satisfaction survey. But in many cases, financial performance is not available at the individual level. In our analysis of survey and financial performance data at "Wolverine Inns" (the name we're using for the hotel chain mentioned in Chapter Two), the solution was to aggregate up to the level of individual hotels or franchisees.

The second issue raises questions about timing. If you want to monitor individual customers' behavior after they have bought a product or used a service, you may have to wait some time before they buy or use the product or service again. The repurchase cycle for a car is three to four years for many consumers—and up to ten years for many others. Companies simply cannot place the quality improvement effort on hold for that long, which is why stated loyalties are often your only proxies for performance.

In situations where outcome data is available and can be tied to satisfaction and loyalty data, the goal is to quantify the links in the framework in Figure 5.1. That is, what are the payoffs of improving performance on attributes and benefits? Allocating resources to optimize customer satisfaction and increase shareholder value requires hard numbers. Importantly, the links must be established on a case-by-case (company-by-company and segment-by-segment) basis.

With Volvo, for example, we find that it is satisfaction rather than loyalty or stated intentions that influences the amount of money customers spend the next time they buy. In many cases such as this, loyalty measures are simply collected too early in the purchase-consumption-repurchase cycle, before customers have formed repurchase plans. In the case of Wolverine Inns, we had to consider the industry-specific role that "location, location, and location" plays in driving hotel performance. Analyzing the data by market segment was also a critical factor.

The tools available to estimate the links to financial performance include PCR (principal-components regression, described earlier) and PLS (partial least squares). If PLS is used, the links are estimated in a single step, which is an advantage when estimating a complex model. PCR is also very useful. As illustrated earlier, it requires running more regression models as more links are established. The primary advantage of PLS is that it explains as much as possible of the variation in the dependent variables, including the behaviors or financial numbers at the end of the chain of causes and effects. This means explaining what drives profit. Once again, however, our experience is that with a good model and good data, any differences between PCR and PLS are minimal.

Figure 5.9 illustrates the logic used when estimating the financial return on improved quality and satisfaction. The logic is similar to a *what-if analysis*, which explores what happens to the outputs of a model when a change is made to the inputs. The idea is to trace the effect of an attribute along the path or paths connecting the attribute to profit.

Consider a 1-unit change in an attribute, for example, the results of an investment that improves performance on the attribute from an 8 to a 9 on the 10-point poor-to-excellent scale. The profit impact of this change equals the impact the attribute has on the benefit in the figure (0.2), times the impact the benefit has on satisfaction (0.5), times the impact that satisfaction has on profit (0.6), times the unstandardized loading on the profit measure (2,300 in dollar units). To get an unstandardized loading, find the corresponding standardized loading, which is simply the correlation between the attribute and the index or latent variable of which it is a part (such as profitability or satisfaction), and which is also available from your principal-components analyses. Then all you need to do is divide the standardized loading by the standard deviation on the attribute. The unstandardized loading serves to translate the profit impact (a stan-

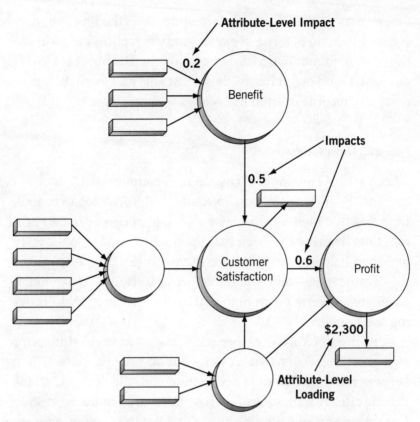

Figure 5.9. The Attribute Impact to Attribute Loading Logic of Financial Profit

dardized, latent variable impact in PCR and PLS) back into one of your original profit measures (profit or revenues in U.S. dollars or Swedish kronor, for example). Thus, the profit from increasing performance on the attribute in Figure 5.9 by one unit is

$$0.2 \times 0.5 \times 0.6 \times 2300 = \$138$$

Costs are incorporated into this type of analysis in two ways. If the financial link in the model is directly to profit, and the link is positive, it implies that the costs typically incurred to increase quality on the attribute are more than covered by increased revenues. Otherwise the link wouldn't be positive! In other cases, such as the Wolverine Inns case, the link is to revenues. When that is so, a separate study is required to estimate the costs required to increase quality on the attribute by a given amount. Good estimates of these costs may be available from company records or from interviews with managers.

Financial Links for Volvo

After years of creating and sustaining a commitment to increasing quality and satisfaction, executives at Volvo began to look for proof that their approach was having an effect on their bottom line. It was not enough that the quality-satisfaction-loyalty logic had helped them to sell a customer orientation throughout the organization—they wanted to prove it. They also wanted to calculate just how much money they were making by improving their quality.

At present Volvo has three different satisfaction studies for customers in Sweden that it carries out on a regular basis. These surveys measure customer satisfaction with the dealer, with the vehicle after two months of ownership, and with the workshop (maintenance and repair shop). The database used here includes information on approximately twenty-five thousand individual customers who bought a Volvo in 1994 and bought a new car again in 1997. The database is unique in that it contains information for some customers on, for instance, whether the second vehicle purchased was another Volvo, whether they used Volvo financing, had Volvo insurance, and possessed a Volvo charge card.

For reasons of confidentiality, we only show analyses conducted using the sales satisfaction survey. A sample of customers was extracted from the database who were truly loyal in that they bought another Volvo ($n = 393$) and for whom profit data was available. It is natural to assume that these customers were relatively satisfied with their previous experience, as can be seen from the satisfaction index for sales (8.73 for the sample compared to 8.56 for the total population in the database based on a 10-point scale). Figure 5.10 presents results from the analysis. The circles to the left in the figure represent benefit areas measured as latent variables from the questionnaire. The variables to the right represent different behaviors (possession of a Volvo card, financing with Volvo, and so on). The numbers within the circles are the performance-level indices for the drivers of satisfaction and the numbers on the arrows represent the impacts.

Performance of the vehicle (very early in the consumption experience) has the highest impact on satisfaction, followed by the performance of the personnel and vehicle delivery respectively. The impact of satisfaction on stated loyalty at the time of the survey is 0.410. Typically, stated loyalty should affect subsequent customer behaviors and profit. However, we found stated loyalty to have no impact on profit in this case. As noted earlier, the loyalty measures in this case are simply collected too early in

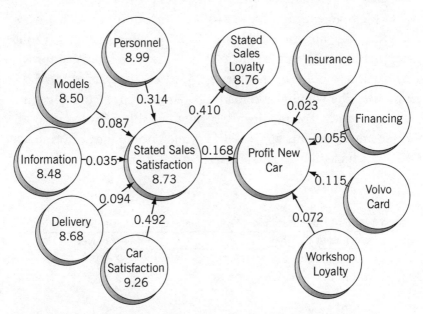

Figure 5.10. Sales Satisfaction Model for Loyal Volvo Customers

the purchase-consumption-repurchase cycle (shortly after delivery), when it is difficult for customers to reflect on their future buying plans and state whether they will buy another Volvo. What is interesting, however, is that overall satisfaction even early in the consumption experience has a very significant and positive impact on profit per customer on the next vehicle purchased.

Volvo managers also wanted to understand the way many of the other services that they provide customers affect the money spent on the next purchase. The model results show, for example, that if a customer uses the Volvo charge card, that usage has a significant positive impact on future profit. Volvo has been successful in providing a financial service through its card, by which the customer can divide any charge into four payments without incurring any additional costs. It may be surprising to find that vehicle financing has a negative effect on profit. The explanation is that salespeople often give customers who finance their cars through Volvo a better price knowing that the company will make more money on the total package.

We then estimated the profit impact of quality improvement in the sales process. Our what-if analysis asked, "What happens if a customer's perceptions of the sales process improve by one scale point in the survey?" A PLS analysis of the data provided the weights and loadings required to calculate the impact on profit. The results are shown in Table 5.3. Note that all these improvements apply without reference to the performance of the vehicle, which is an entirely separate matter.

Table 5.3. Estimated Return on Quality Improvements in the Sales Process

Latent Variable	Percent of Net
Personnel	2.7
Available Models	0.5
Information	0.2
Delivery	0.6

We found that if the Volvo dealers improved their quality one scale point on each of the four areas in the table (based on 10-point performance scales), they gained roughly 4 percent more profit downstream at the next purchase. They gained most by improving personnel (almost 3 percent). Although not shown here, it is possible to break this effect down into improvements on specific attributes of the customer-salesperson interaction. The analysis provides a flavor of the types of impacts that can be determined when survey data and profit per customer data is combined. Most interesting is that the customer data in this example, which is collected up to three years prior to the sale of the next vehicle, predicts significant positive effects on future profit.

Financial Links for Wolverine Inns

Our second example comes from the hotel industry. As noted earlier, we refer to the hotel chain in the example as "Wolverine Inns" to preserve confidentiality, and we have changed some of the results. Our database includes quality and satisfaction data for several hundred of the chain's properties across North America. This data was combined with the financial performance data for each hotel. Thus an "observation" in this case is an individual hotel rather than an individual customer (just as the Sears model in Chapter One focused on individual stores rather than individual customers). The "lens of the customer" and model used to establish the financial links is shown in Figure 5.11.

The quality areas feeding into satisfaction represent different attribute groupings in the hotel chain's survey. Two to three weeks after their hotel stay, customers receive a written questionnaire that they fill out and return to the company. The database also includes several control variables, including the age of the hotel rooms, the number of rooms, and penetration rate (average occupancy rates relative to local competitors). These control variables were included because they have some small but

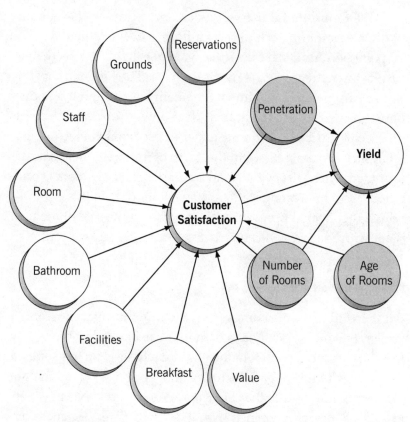

Figure 5.11. Quality, Satisfaction, and Yield at Wolverine Inns

systematic effects on the dependent variables (where, for example, satisfaction is slightly lower for larger hotels with older rooms).

An interesting aspect of this analysis is that when quality and satisfaction were used in an attempt to explain profit measures for the various hotels (gross profit, revenues, operating costs), we essentially found that they had no effects. Recognizing that each industry is unique, we realized that our problem was that the analysis did not control for the overriding effects of "location, location, location" when explaining hotel performance. The solution was to link satisfaction directly to yield. *Yield* is a measure of the revenues generated per available room relative to direct competitors in a given location. Once yield was used in the analysis, very predictable effects of quality and satisfaction improvement were observed. The effects were also very dependent on location type, which we used as a proxy for market segment.

The six location types for the hotel chain were airport, downtown (in larger cities), leisure-area (in vacation spots), roadside, small market, and suburban. Impact-performance charts for the downtown and leisure-area properties were illustrated back in Chapter Two. The different locations are interesting in that we expect the payoff from quality and satisfaction improvement to vary systematically across the location types. The payback should be greatest in those segments where customers have abundant choices and repeat the purchase-repurchase cycle on a regular basis, such as in downtown and airport locations. We expect the effects to be much lower where customers have little choice among hotels. For roadside locations, for example, customers are more likely to be transient or one-time visitors and the competition is limited. When it is late, the kids are tired, and there is a room available, people tend to live by the maxim "beggars can't be choosers" and take whatever they get. Figure 5.12 presents the estimated impact on yield from the model across the six different property types.

The results were very consistent with our predictions. Satisfaction has its greatest effects on yield where competition is greatest, in the airport, downtown, and leisure-area locations. The effects are smaller for the other properties. For the roadside locations, where the hostage situation is greatest, the effect is actually negative (albeit nonsignificant) suggesting that the chain has essentially optimized satisfaction with respect to generating revenues there. In every other location the effect remains positive and significant. For the downtown properties, increasing satisfaction by one unit has a 0.3 impact on yield (a standardized impact).

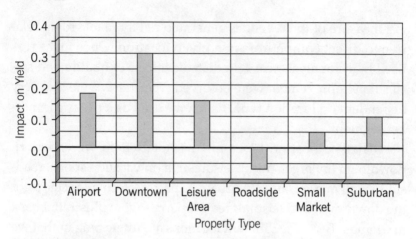

Figure 5.12. Impact of Improving Satisfaction on Yield Across Property Types

We still needed to translate the impacts on yield into dollars. This was again done using a what-if analysis. We asked the question, "What if satisfaction is improved by 0.1 scale points in the survey?" The scale in this case in a 5-point scale, where the values on satisfaction across properties typically ranged from 4.0 to 4.6. The increase thus represents improvements in satisfaction in the customer base from, for example, 4.3 to 4.4 or 4.4 to 4.5 on the satisfaction scale. The increase is one that we found both the hotel chain's management and hotel owners could understand from a cost standpoint.

Here's how we then translated the 0.1 scale point changes into revenue dollars. We knew the number of rooms in each hotel and the average room rates. Multiplying the number of rooms (say 100) times the occupancy rates (say 80 percent), times the days of the year the room is available (365), times the average daily rate (say $60 dollars per room) provides an estimated net revenue from the "sale of rooms" of $1,752,000. When the estimated impact on yield percentage is considered, such as an unstandardized impact of 10 percent, we know to increase the room rate by that amount (from $60 per room to $66). The increase in yield changes the revenues on room sales to $1,927,200, which represents an increase in revenues for the property of $175,200. The estimated increases in revenue for a 0.1 scale-point improvement in satisfaction are shown in Figure 5.13.

The results suggest that the satisfaction increase raises revenues by approximately $160,000 per hotel for the downtown locations and by over $50,000 per hotel for the airport locations. The effects are much lower where the impacts are lower. The results are important for at least two reasons. First, they illustrate the importance of performing such analyses on a market segment level. Averaging across property types would be very misleading in this case. Second, the segment-level results emphasize the importance of optimizing as opposed to maximizing satisfaction. It appears that satisfaction is more or less optimized in those cases where competition is limited and customers are in a hostage situation. In contrast, where competition is abundant and repeat patronage is strong (such as for business travelers visiting downtown locations), further increases in satisfaction will continue to generate revenues.

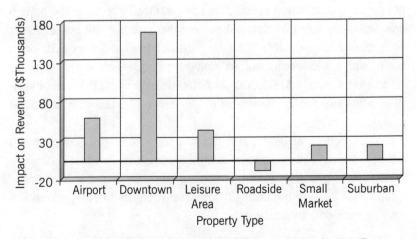

Figure 5.13. Impact of Improving Satisfaction on Revenues Across Property Types

CHAPTER SUMMARY

Statistical estimates of attribute and benefit impact are worth the effort because they are superior to self-rated importance measures at distinguishing impact—the effect that a change in quality has on satisfaction and subsequent loyalty. Among the statistical methods, only some leverage understanding of the lens of the customer. Two methods, our variation on principal-components regression (PCR) and partial least squares (PLS), use the attribute and benefit categories established in earlier qualitative research to develop benefit indices, reduce cross-correlation in customers' perceptions, and provide meaningful statistical impacts for the attributes and benefits.

Analyzing customer data through the lens of the customer provides tremendous insight into just what benefits and attributes have the greatest impact on customers' consumption experiences. Although the approaches are somewhat complex, they are necessary to provide the best possible information for input to the priority-setting process. At the same time, we hope we have given you a straightforward process for implementing PCR. We recommend the PCR approach as a cost-effective way of using off-the-shelf statistical software to analyze the lens of the customer. If you've developed a strong customer lens, constructed a good questionnaire, and collected high-quality survey data, any differences between our PCR approach and PLS should be insignificant.

When financial data is added to a satisfaction model, the impacts of improving quality and satisfaction can be traced directly to the bottom line. Volvo, for example, saw a 4 percent increase in profit per customer on future sales due solely to higher satisfaction (1 point on a 10-point scale) with the sales process. At Wolverine Inns, revenues increased by up to approximately $160,000 per hotel, depending on the type of location, when satisfaction increased by one-tenth of a point (on a 5-point scale).

But models, analyses, and impact and performance scores should not be confused with the decisions that managers make when setting priorities and targeting changes that need to be made. In our sixth and final chapter we take up the critically important role that managers take in moving from data to decisions.

Questions for Consideration

1. How strong is the quality of the analysis applied to your quality, customer satisfaction, and loyalty data? Based on what you've read here, how could your analysis be improved?

2. What is your experience with nonlinear relationships in quality, customer satisfaction, and loyalty data? How does your company interpret and deal with such relationships?

3. Describe your company's market segmentation scheme and how it was developed. Do you use this scheme to guide your quality-satisfaction-loyalty data analysis, or is it the result of your analysis? What are the strengths and weaknesses of your segmentation scheme?

4. Does your customer data analysis link quality, satisfaction, or loyalty to bottom-line financial performance? If not, what would it take in terms of data requirements and analysis to do so?

From Information to Decisions

Priority Setting and Implementation

Once you've built the lens of the customer for your products or services and seen the valuable information it can help you produce, it's tempting to sit back and ask, "Well, now what do the numbers say we should do?"

But it's not that simple. The critical next phase of the process is to use the information to set priorities for improvement. And don't underestimate the importance of obtaining top management input to your action plans at this point. This may require some persistence. Too often managers view measurement systems, including the quality-satisfaction-loyalty model we present here, as a means of avoiding tough decisions—but "the numbers" don't pay the bills, and they don't make decisions, either.

Managers who are in charge of implementing their company's strategies and hold the authority to budget and who allocate resources to improve quality and satisfaction cannot absent themselves from the process. The numbers simply help managers base their decisions on facts.

Here in this chapter we close the loop. We first discuss management's role in using the output of the measurement system to set priorities for improvement. We then discuss how to implement the priorities. We bridge the gap between the customer benefits and product or service attributes that need improvement and the internal changes they require.

■ Set Priorities

As we said in Chapter One, setting priorities requires both impact and performance information for the various drivers of satisfaction and loyalty. But to set priorities, you must make some critical decisions regarding just what constitutes high versus low impact and high versus low performance. These decisions require you to consider a number of factors beyond the information in your impact-performance chart, including your strategy and competencies as well as relevant benchmarks, costs, and market dynamics.

Start with the Strategic Satisfaction Matrix

The starting point for your analysis is the strategic satisfaction matrix introduced in Chapter One and presented again as Figure 6.1. Recall that the basic logic is to categorize the various benefit and attribute drivers of satisfaction into one of the four cells of the matrix, each of which is associated with its own market action implications. Generally, the essential areas to improve are those where impact or importance is high and performance

Low Impact and Strong Performance: Maintain or reduce investment or alter target market	High Impact and Strong Performance: Maintain or improve performance— Competitive advantage
Low Impact and Weak Performance: Inconsequential— Do not waste resources	High Impact and Weak Performance: Focus improvements here—Competitive vulnerability

Figure 6.1. Strategic Satisfaction Matrix

is low. Customers are essentially telling us that we are falling short in these important areas. Improvements to these areas will effectively focus resources where they have the greatest impact on satisfaction and subsequent loyalty and profitability. This is also the cell in which you are most competitively vulnerable. If competitors do an excellent job in these areas, they will lure your customers away.

Those areas that are important to customers and in which your performance is strong represent your core competencies and competitive advantages. It is essential to maintain if not improve performance on these drivers. The implications for the opposite cell, where impact is low and performance is weak, are also clear. Generally, there's no reason to waste resources on improving these areas. According to the customers, performance here just doesn't matter.

The implications for the remaining cell, in which impact is low yet performance is high, are less straightforward. This may be an area where resources have been wasted in the past because the benefits and attributes are not important to customers. In one recent application, for example, we found that customers at an IKEA furniture store in the United States rated traditional

Swedish amenities—a child-care facility and a Swedish bake-shop—very positively. Nonetheless, these amenities had little to no impact on satisfaction and loyalty. From a cost-benefit stand-point, we concluded that having the amenities was not cost-effective for the U.S.-based store.

Alternatively, benefits and attributes in the low impact–high performance category may contain drivers of satisfaction that customers consider to be basic and necessary (as in Kano's model described in Chapter Five). Customers may find these benefits and attributes everywhere they look and take them for granted. Although important in an absolute sense, these features offer no differentiation because there is little to no variance in their performance across customers and competitors. Airline safety is a classic example here—as long as the planes aren't falling out of the sky, passengers tend to regard one airline as much the same as another. That doesn't mean that any airline can afford to ease off on safety! The same sort of consideration can apply in less dramatic circumstances as well. In the IKEA project, we found that "ease of assembly" was also rated highly and had little impact. Our conclusion here, however, was to make certain that we assure continued high performance on this benefit. Withdrawing resources and reducing performance would only serve to put us on a "slippery slope" and decrease satisfaction. The area would quickly return to the high im-pact–low performance category. Another possibility in the high performance–low impact quadrant is to find a new target mar-ket segment for the product or service. It may well be possible to find new customers who would especially value these bene-fit areas (such as customers who would value the child-care and bakery facilities in the IKEA store).

But data analysis does not determine where to draw the cell boundaries. Managers must draw the lines and decide just where the improvement should occur. Again, the impact-performance charts are a primary input to this decision process, but there are several other factors that you need to consider.

Pay Attention to Strategies and Competencies

Your strategic market plan leads you to focus on particular segments of customers to leverage core competencies. But what if your customer data analysis suggests that you improve in areas that are inconsistent with your basic strengths? Management must decide whether or not the areas that need improvement are those in which core competencies and a competitive advantage can be achieved. If not, you may be pursuing customers you can't please with your strengths, at the risk of alienating customers who currently value your offerings. Perhaps you should reconsider your entire strategic market plan instead.

At the same time, the information may be very valuable in deciding on network partners who can help provide customers with the benefits they need. Think back to the convenience store survey, which revealed that safety is the primary driver of satisfaction for customers. In practical terms, safety is not something that a convenience store can completely control, so the implication may be to network and collaborate with those who can have more effect. In some cities, for example, convenience stores provide an area where local law enforcement officers can take a break, make phone calls, and do paperwork. This win-win solution saves the officers time and creates a greater atmosphere of safety than the stores could provide on their own.

Benchmark Impact and Performance

It is also critically important to benchmark both impact and performance when using this information to set priorities. In the Råtorp Tire Company case (Appendix A at the back of the book), impact-performance charts are supplied for three main competitors in the market. As the reader quickly finds out, making decisions for Råtorp requires a careful consideration of impact and performance levels for the competitors as well. In an absolute sense, impact may be high and performance low in a given area, suggesting the need to make improvements. But what if your closest competitor shows even lower performance and higher impact? It may be a mistake to improve that area if there are others that also call for attention. Relatively, it may be a competitive strength, at least in the short run.

At the same time, do not ignore the absolute levels of impact and performance. Over the long haul, the absolute levels of performance and impact highlight your vulnerabilities, as well as those of your competitors, and suggest where new competitors may enter or improve to take customers away.

Involve Management in Considering Costs

In Chapter Five we briefly discussed how to incorporate cost considerations into the analysis. When you tie your model and analysis to increased profit per customer, you then have some idea that the costs typically incurred to improve quality are covered. But in most cases, managers must consider the relative costs of making improvements when deciding which areas to improve. Remember that the goal is to optimize rather than maximize satisfaction and loyalty. If two areas show equally low performance and high impact, managers should ask, "Which is more cost-effective to improve?" One source of cost information is management itself. Another is through the use of tools such as QFD (quality function deployment, described later in this chapter) that translate product improvements into internal change and explicitly consider cost information.

Ask Where the Market Is Heading

Finally, consider where your market is headed over time. Just what factors will become more or less important? For personal computers, will processing speed become less of a differential advantage going forward? For convenience stores, will prepared foods become a greater source of differentiation and impact? Both social and technological forecasting are important bases for predicting these market dynamics, but are beyond the scope of our discussion.

■ Returning to Råtorp

Appendix A at the end of the book concludes with a priority-setting exercise that makes use of the Råtorp Tire Company information discussed in Chapter Three. The exercise provides the output of a survey and data analysis for Råtorp and its two main competitors. We strongly encourage you to work through the data in the case and set priorities for Råtorp. Based on the data, consider what you expect the competition to do as well. The case will force you to consider several factors, including what Råtorp's strategy should be, how the benchmarks influence interpretation of the results, how the competition is likely to evolve over time (such as the role filled by import brands), and what the improvements might cost. The case emphasizes that the task of moving from information to decisions is far from trivial. It requires significant reflection and input from managers in a position to set and implement a strategic market plan.

■ Bridge the Quality-Satisfaction Gap

Once you have targeted which benefits and attributes to improve, you have to figure out just how to improve them. In effect, you need to build a bridge from your model of customer perceptions and behaviors to your internal metrics, parts, processes, and people. When you do this, you'll soon find that—as with any bridge—the traffic on this one flows both ways.

The Gustafsson and Johnson Framework

This discussion draws heavily on a quality-satisfaction framework that the authors recently developed, which is presented in Figure 6.2.[1] The framework integrates aspects of two leading approaches to improving quality and satisfaction: *quality function deployment* (QFD) and customer satisfaction modeling (as detailed in Chapter Five). Together, the two approaches illustrate qualitatively different steps in the overall process of translating satisfaction into its means of accomplishment. Our satisfaction models translate overall satisfaction down into the customer benefits that drive satisfaction and into the product and service attributes that provide the benefits. These are the uppermost stages of the framework. The lower stages, taken from QFD, translate these attributes further down into their means of accomplishment or production.

It is important to consider what we mean by *translation* in the framework. Consistent with the arrows in the figure, translation is a process of moving from the most abstract information of interest to the most concrete. Customer satisfaction is customers' overall evaluation of their purchase and consumption experience. Moving downstream in the framework from satisfaction to production is, therefore, a process of translating abstract, subjective evaluations into concrete, objective means of accomplishment.

In contrast, the process of moving up in the framework from concrete processes and attributes to abstract benefits and overall satisfaction is more of an inductive or *change monitoring* process. After determining what changes to make, it is important to track the changes back upstream in the process. Did, for

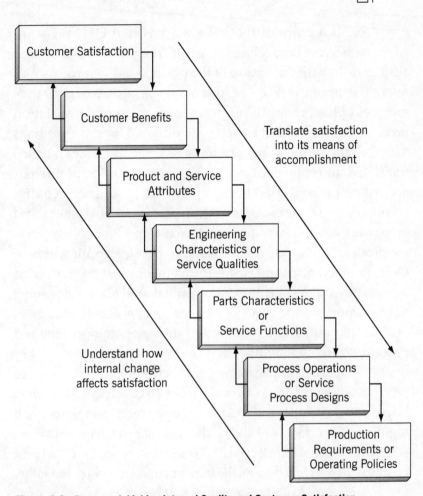

Figure 6.2. Framework Linking Internal Quality and Customer Satisfaction

example, the changes we made internally have a subsequent effect on customer perceptions and satisfaction? To what degree did our improvements to production processes improve process operations, parts deployment, engineering or design characteristics, and ultimately attribute and benefit performance? As the figure shows, the combination of translation and change monitoring forms a two-way traffic that is essential to close the loop on the quality improvement process.

A central point of the framework is that QFD picks up where satisfaction modeling leaves off. The product and service attributes that are the output of the priority-setting process represent the input to QFD. The four houses or phases of QFD thus represent phases four through seven of an overall translation process. The translation is, however, different for pure products than for pure services. For products, targeted attributes must be translated into engineering or design characteristics, parts characteristics, process operations, and finally production requirements. Because services are co-produced by customers and employees at a time and place of the customer's choosing, service production is a different beast. In service applications of QFD, targeted attributes for improvement must be translated into service qualities (for example, hotel arrival), service functions (airport shuttle service), service process designs (number of shuttles, routes, and personnel), and operating policies and procedures (daily schedules and contingency plans).[2]

An important implication of the framework is that for a given product or service, there are at least seven conceptually distinct stages in the overall translation and change monitoring process. It highlights the difficulties and challenges that we face even after a satisfaction model is analyzed and priorities are set. Our goal here is not to exhaustively discuss the implementation phases, but rather to introduce you to QFD as one tool that has helped thousands of companies around the world to link their customer data to product and service improvements. A thorough treatment of how tools such as QFD are used to implement product-driven product and process changes is beyond the scope of this book. It is, in fact, the subject of our next book in the UMBS Management Series.

Use Quality Function Deployment

QFD is mainly a tool to help companies focus on what customers perceive as important and certify that these desired abilities exist in the final product or service. The work is usually documented in a series of matrices. Its primary benefits are reduced design costs and development time. Other benefits include improving communication and cohesion within a product development or improvement team and solidifying design decisions early in the development cycle.

Generally there are two variants of the QFD methodology. The first is the four-phase system captured as part of Figure 6.2 and presented in more detail in Figure 6.3 (illustrated using traditional product-based QFD). In this approach, QFD starts with an input list of customer-desired attributes. These attributes are often ordered hierarchically to handle the large number required to describe a product (such as an automobile door system). At a higher level of abstraction are the benefit categories similar to those used in our satisfaction model (such as that a door system "operates well"). At a lower level of abstraction are the more concrete attributes (such as that a door system is "easy to close from the outside").

The QFD translation process begins in Phase 1, the "House of Quality,"[3] where attributes are translated into engineering characteristics. In subsequent phases—often called *houses*— engineering targets are translated into parts characteristics; targeted parts characteristics are translated into key process operations; and key process operations are translated into production requirements or work instructions. (As mentioned, this system is altered when applied to services.)

The second variant of QFD recognizes that the four-phase system in Figure 6.3 only fulfills a portion of the planning that is needed for a new product. Separate matrix systems are required to incorporate product quality deployment, technology deployment, cost deployment, and reliability deployment throughout the planning, design, trial, manufacturing, and service phases of product development and launch.[4] Because, however, the two variants are essentially similar and the four-phase

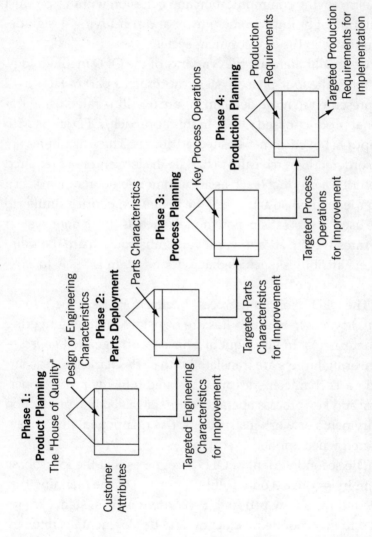

Phase 1:
Product Planning
The "House of Quality"

Design or Engineering
Characteristics

Customer
Attributes

Targeted Engineering
Characteristics
for Improvement

Phase 2:
Parts Deployment

Parts Characteristics

Targeted Parts
Characteristics
for Improvement

Phase 3:
Process Planning

Key Process Operations

Targeted Process
Operations
for Improvement

Phase 4:
Production Planning

Production
Requirements

Targeted Production
Requirements for
Implementation

Figure 6.3. The Four Phases of Traditional Product QFD

system in Figure 6.3 is better known and easier to grasp, it will be used to illustrate the QFD approach.

Phase One: The House of Quality

Whatever the variant, the QFD process begins with the voice of the customer. Once "customer needs" are translated into benefit and attribute priorities, the attributes become the input to the House of Quality. The House of Quality, illustrated in Figure 6.4, is used to understand the voice of the customer and translate it into the voice of the engineer.

Like quality-satisfaction-loyalty modeling, QFD is a focusing tool that strives to make efficient use of a company's limited resources. This focusing or priority setting again requires importance measures for the desired product or service attributes. Customer input is also used in the market evaluation section to benchmark how the product or service of interest performs on

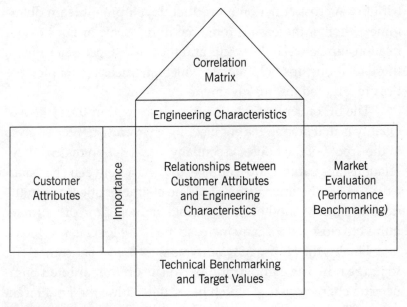

Figure 6.4. The House of Quality

the attributes in question, often relative to immediate competitors. Ideally the attribute importance and performance information used in QFD comes directly from the preceding analysis of satisfaction. Priority targets are set or quality resources are deployed to improve those attributes that are important to customers and on which the product is performing poorly relative to competitors.

The next task is to determine the *hows;* that is, how the *whats* (the customer attributes) are to be fulfilled through engineering or design characteristics. These characteristics should be expressed in measurable terms (such as the amount of pressure required to close a door from the outside) and a target value should be given to each attribute. It is important to point out that the engineering characteristics are not design solutions, which come in the second matrix or house. There are two types of relationships specified in the House of Quality. The first is that between the engineering characteristics and the customer attributes. A cross-functional product development team determines whether there is a strong, medium, weak, or nonexistent relationship between the whats and the hows. Once determined, these relationships help dictate which engineering characteristics are targeted for improvement.

The other type of relationship described in the House of Quality is that among the engineering characteristics themselves in the "roof" of the house. Essentially a correlation matrix, these relationships capture any conflicts that exist between characteristics, where the improvement of one characteristic leads to the deterioration of another (for example, reducing the pressure required to close a door may increase the noise level in a vehicle).

Finally, the House of Quality uses technical benchmarking to judge how the competition performs on the targeted engineering characteristics, which helps determine the final target values. This is another stage in the overall translation where cost information is critical in determining the targets.

Phases Two, Three, and Four

Subsequent phases in the QFD process ensure that areas with a high impact on customer satisfaction are controlled throughout the production or service delivery process. In Phase Two the information received about engineering characteristics is transformed into different parts of the product. Targeted hows from the first matrix are used as input and become the whats in the second matrix. The design process, the fitting of form to function, occurs between Phase One and Phase Two. In Phase Three, process planning, decisions are made about how different parts will be manufactured. In Phase Four, or production planning, instructions on how to manufacture the product are developed. In the case of a service, process charts may be used to describe the desired service delivery so that service personnel know what they should do to consistently provide a high quality of service.

CHAPTER SUMMARY

The lens of the customer and the survey, data, and analyses that result provide a wealth of information—but no decisions. Customer information is only input to the decisions that managers make to drive change in their company. Meanwhile, improving product or service performance is itself a complex translation that runs from attributes down to the production instructions and operating policies that employees use.

Making decisions and driving change are both tasks that are easier said than done. As a manager you bring a wealth of knowledge to the information that emerges from a quality-satisfaction-loyalty model and analysis, all of which helps to decide just which quality changes can and should be made. With that decision made, tools such as QFD help you to bridge the gap between internal quality and external quality and satisfaction by breaking the process down into a series of steps that translate the lens of the customer into the lens of the organization.

Once you have closed the loop from building the lens of the customer to setting priorities and implementing change, it is time to begin the process anew. A customer orientation is a continuous process of understanding customer needs, disseminating information throughout the organization, and following through to make changes that improve satisfaction and profitability. The key is to view quality, satisfaction, or loyalty not as passing fads but as essential factors in driving bottom-line profits. Because competition only increases over time, the choices for management are clear. Die a slow death or generate long-term profits by giving customers the constant attention that they deserve.

Questions for Consideration

1. Now that we have closed the loop in our discussion of customer measurement and management systems, reevaluate your own system. What specific recommendation would you make to improve the system?
2. Does your company use QFD or some other tool to translate customer needs into their means of accomplishment? If so, what are the strengths and weaknesses of your approach? If not, how do you implement the recommended changes that emerge from your customer satisfaction measurement system?
3. What are the keys to moving the customer orientation process forward in your company?

Appendix A

Råtorp Tire Company

This appendix provides background information and exercises based on the authors' experience with a major manufacturer of tires. Section 1 presents the protocol that served as a guideline for conducting interviews in conjunction with the customer satisfaction study performed for that manufacturer, here referred to as "Råtorp Tire Company." The protocol covers the most important steps of the "critical incident technique" (CIT) described in Chapter Three. Section 2 is an exercise for Chapter Three, while Section 3 is an exercise for Chapter Six.

■ 1. Sample CIT Interview Protocol

At the beginning of the interview, describe to the interviewee the nature and goals of the research that Råtorp is conducting. More specifically, inform the retailer/wholesaler how important the

Note: Professor Michael D. Johnson of the University of Michigan Business School prepared this case study. The case is intended as a learning exercise rather than to illustrate either effective or ineffective handling of a situation. The company names and the data in the case have been changed to preserve confidentiality.

study is for both the retailer/wholesaler and Råtorp. The motivation is to improve the relationship between Råtorp and the retailer/wholesaler by solving problems and making changes in the way Råtorp interacts with its retailers/wholesalers to improve their satisfaction and the profitability of their businesses. Assure the retailer/wholesaler of the integrity and anonymity of this survey. They should feel completely free to say anything they want. We guarantee that this information will be kept totally anonymous.

After the introduction, ask the retailer/wholesaler to list the things they "like" and then the things they "dislike" about their interaction with Råtorp. Based on pretests of the interview protocol, it is clear that the number of "dislikes" generally exceeds the number of "likes." Therefore, we recommend giving a range for the number of responses they should provide. Also, start with the "likes" before moving to the "dislikes" (unless the respondent insists on moving directly to the "dislikes"). We recommend a range of "5 to 10" responses for each category (likes and dislikes). This range should only serve as a guideline. In our pretests, respondents had little trouble filling this quota for "dislikes." If the respondent has trouble coming up with at least 5 "likes," feel free to move on to the "dislikes." If, on the other hand, the respondent has no problem coming up with more than 10 "likes" or 10 "dislikes," don't stop the respondent.

Where it seems appropriate, ask the respondent about the positive benefits or negative consequences of particular "likes" and "dislikes." If, for example, the benefit or consequence of an incident is unclear ("Råtorp fails to inform me about coming price changes"), you might ask, "Why is that important to you?" or "How does that affect you?" This information will later help us to categorize the critical incidents by benefit or consequence category. Where, in contrast, an incident is too general ("The service is good"), it would also be appropriate to probe for more detail. For example, you might ask, "What do you mean by good service?"

For a successful application of the CIT it is very important to keep in mind what exactly a "critical incident" is. *A critical incident is a specific example of the service or product that describes either positive or negative performance.* A good critical incident has two characteristics: (1) it is specific, and (2) it describes the service provider in behavioral terms or describes the service or product with specific adjectives. As a consequence of this characterization, you should probe for more details if the answer of the interviewee is too general.

Finish the interview by first asking if there is anything else about their interactions with Råtorp on which the retailer/ wholesaler would like to comment. Also, are there particular things they would like to see changed or improved? Finally, thank the respondent for participating and provide them with some timetable for the research. For example, say that Råtorp will use the information to produce a more formal satisfaction survey for the entire retailer/wholesaler network, which the respondent should receive by a certain date.

■ 2. Reader Exercise for Chapter Three

This exercise presents detailed interview results that were obtained using the critical incident technique with Råtorp Tire Company.

Background

In an effort to improve its customer orientation, the Råtorp Tire Company has undertaken a systematic study of the drivers of customer satisfaction and loyalty for replacement tires in its home market. Its initial focus is on intermediate customers in the channel of distribution (wholesalers and retailers). This is because over 70 percent of replacement tires are purchased based on recommendations from a retailer. The specific goal of the research is to build a model of the drivers of satisfaction and loyalty for Råtorp's most important customers, the ones who "push" the product out to the end users. The research uses a set of structured interviews to determine the distributors' requirements in the form of product and service attributes and benefits that drive their satisfaction and subsequent loyalty.

This report summarizes a subset of the results from the initial qualitative interviews conducted for Råtorp. The focus is on interviews conducted with a representative sample of dealers from "Galileo," an independent chain of retailers that installs and services replacement tires. These retailers were each administered a formal CIT (Critical Incident Technique) interview. Each retailer was asked to describe specific "likes" and "dislikes" about the products and services provided by Råtorp. When the answers were too general the interviewers were instructed to probe deeper to get more specific responses. Likewise, when it seemed appropriate, interviewers asked respondents to indicate the consequences or benefits of their experiences. The spreadsheets that follow list examples of the positive and negative incidents raised by the retailers as well as responses to the probes administered for each critical incident.

Problem

Your task is to cluster the critical incidents into satisfaction attributes and then group the attributes into more general benefit categories or clusters. These attributes, organized by benefit category, are to be used as survey measures in a customer satisfaction survey and model. If a group of individuals is conducting the analysis, discuss any discrepancies perceived among members of the group and develop a master list. A CIT worksheet is included at the back of the case to facilitate your analysis and discussion.

Positive Incidents	*Detailed Comments and Responses to Probing Questions*
They provide a good supply.	It keeps me from having to have a large inventory given the large number of sizes I must sell. I also keep from being stuck with a large stock of tires that does not sell, which frees up my capital.
The prices are attractive.	Before, my clients associated Råtorp with being cheap. They still offer a good price, but now both quality and price are higher.
I like the advertising materials.	They provide leaflets, posters, flags, banners, gadgets, pens, and other materials. I like to give them to the kids when their daddy comes to buy tires. It reflects nicely on me and helps advertise the products outside the store.
The range of products is good.	Råtorp offers a tire for almost every customer that walks in my store. When we call, they also know right away whether they have the tire in stock.
Their information is reliable.	I can count on what they tell me about the tires, what is in stock and when they will be here. They give us good information on what kinds of tires are available in markets here and elsewhere. It keeps me up to date and I know what to tell my clients.
I get the tires quickly.	I can call on the phone and get the tires within 24 hours. This lets me make smaller orders. I make more frequent payments, but they are smaller.

Positive Incidents	*Detailed Comments and Responses to Probing Questions*
Advertising materials are provided.	I like the booklets they provide. I give them to my customers and they have something more than just tires to take home. They can read them and learn something more.
Good cooperation with the truck tire division.	There are few formalities, which I like. The orders do not have to be of a fixed size and the boss is not too busy to call me to ask how my sales are. I order on the phone and the tires are delivered. They also learn pretty quickly just what tires are selling.
Organized training sessions.	My workers learn a lot from these. We are better able to explain to the customers just what is going on and how their tires will work on their vehicles.
The tires are not bad.	I have few complaints about the tires. I am satisfied with the quality. Customers trust the tires and there is a good chance they will return.
They provide materials for events.	Råtorp often has events such as national rallies that I sponsor, where customers can win free tires. They provide flags, banners, caps, and other gadgets for the events. The National Tire people say they are not interested in such small events, but they are fun for our customers.
Effective cooperation with the wholesale house.	Because the cooperation is good, I have at least three places I can order tires from and all three of them deliver. In winter there was a shortage

Positive Incidents	*Detailed Comments and Responses to Probing Questions*
	of tires. But I was able to call here and there and collect what I needed.
Fair financial cooperation with wholesale house.	I have been working with these guys for ten years, and they don't charge me with interest if I am just a bit late with my payments. The factory is not so good—they charge me right away. Cash flow is sometimes a problem.
The products are good.	I have no complaints regarding the quality, for both car and truck tires. The range of tires and treads has been considerably extended. Almost every customer can find what he or she wants.
The winter tires are good.	They have finally produced a decent winter tire. Customers in our market believe strongly in switching to winter tires, which is great for me.
Regional "guardian angel."	The regional representative is very nice. He solves problems for me right away, I don't have to send four or five faxes. He stops by from time to time just to see how things are going. He also offers some training, as in marketing. I have been sending my workers, and would like to go there myself. These guys are important because they give direct feedback to Råtorp.
No problems with deliveries.	They used to come and just give us what they had. Now they come and give us what we need. Råtorp is the best at doing this.

Positive Incidents	*Detailed Comments and Responses to Probing Questions*
Effective cooperation with sales representative.	He comes often. I can't complain.
Complaints are considered without problems.	I mean, they are handled very fast. And there are even fewer complaints than I get about the foreign tires. Råtorp tires are simply more durable; they have higher mileage.
Good advertising campaign.	It encourages customers to buy. They support their tires with press, radio, and television ads. This creates greater interest, and more customers are beginning to ask about the tires.

Negative Incidents	*Detailed Comments and Responses to Probing Questions*
I have no stands to put tires on.	It would be nice to have two stands, one for inside and one for outside, to display the tires. I have a nice big stand from National Tires. If the product is not displayed, it does not sell as well.
Clients wait a long time for complaints to be considered.	Two weeks is too long, and I have to give spare tires then. And the client blames me, not Råtorp. But my point of service is not to blame.
They do not provide commissions for good and large retailers.	They should provide a 2–3 percent discount for better retailers. Too many small, poor-quality stores can buy Råtorp tires and sell them, which reflects badly on the company.

Detailed Comments and Responses

Negative Incidents | *to Probing Questions*

Products are delivered by an agent. | Råtorp should deliver their own tires. The agent takes some percent and my income is lowered.

Sometimes, the people who deliver are not well mannered. | They smoke and keep their hands in their pockets during conversation. I mind it personally, as I don't smoke myself.

Quality of the tires. | Råtorp tires used to have some problems. If a client bought them in the past and had problems, they will not buy them again.

I get too few gadgets, and not what I want. | I get too few advertising materials, and the clients don't want them. They say they are ugly. Some Råtorp clothes for my people would be nice also. We get clothes from National on a regular basis and it makes a good impression on the clients.

The payment terms are too short. | We sell over 20,000 tires a year and get no break on our payment terms. I get better terms from National.

The deliveries are irregular. | You never know when the product is going to come. We can not afford that. The product must be there when we need it.

I have problems with the information they provide. | Råtorp needs to tell us how long a tire will be sold so we are careful how we sell it. We don't want to mislead our clients that a tire will be available and then it is not.

Negative Incidents	*Detailed Comments and Responses to Probing Questions*
No discounts for sales and installation.	Other manufacturers offer discounts based on quantity. The ability to get discounts should depend on the number of tires installed.
I can not fix clear complaints on the spot.	All complaints that are not controversial should be solved at once. This would make it easier to talk to clients, increase satisfaction, and increase the chances that they will buy Råtorp again.
There are gaps in the assortment.	They do not offer me all tires, especially new models for Western cars. When I don't have a full assortment, I don't sell. I should at least get all the tires in the catalogue.
Regional representative arrives too seldom.	He only comes around every six months. He should come every month, like the Euro Special representative, who stops by often just to see how things are going.
When I order a big supply, the payment should be prolonged.	We currently have a very short payment period, which limits my order volume.
The regional storage employees are incompetent.	The people who serve us from the storehouses do not treat us like clients. Deliveries don't arrive, I don't have tires, I don't sell tires, I don't make money, and I am irritated.
There is a lack of two-way communication.	When they run out of something, I find out about it when the transport arrives and it is missing. If they just told me ahead of time, I might fill the delivery with another tire at another price.

Negative Incidents	*Detailed Comments and Responses to Probing Questions*
It is not clear who is responsible for unloading the tires.	I went to get a delivery that arrived from Råtorp, and the guy who arrived told me to unload it. I told him it was his job to unload it. It should be clear who is responsible for doing what.
Transports arrive too seldom.	During certain seasons, I need more deliveries for certain tires, especially in spring (from March to May) and before winter (from October to December). Last year I had to get some of my stock for this period from somewhere else.
The procedure for dealing with complaints is complicated.	It takes a lot of time, you need to see the tire, and if there is any problem (where a complaint is not accepted), you need to keep the tire until the client comes back to pick it up.
The motivation to sell Råtorp tires is weak.	The motivation for selling tires should be greater and should depend on the sales volume.
They give interest notes (penalties).	If you are late even one or two days, they penalize you. This shouldn't happen, as it is often the bank's fault anyway. I should get five to seven days counted before I am charged interest.
Lack of advertising gadgets for truck drivers.	There should be more for truck drivers, produced especially for them, such as key rings, caps, labels, pins, or bottle openers. They would automatically promote the company all over.

Negative Incidents	*Detailed Comments and Responses to Probing Questions*
The leaflets are not well thought out.	It is embarrassing to show clients flyers for old tires. Clients make decisions and then you have to tell them "they don't make that one anymore."
Dishonest warehouse activities.	Some warehouses lower the prices for Råtorp tires. They need to obey the sales agreements. We end up competing at a retail level directly with our own warehouses.
No information about charges and plans.	National sometimes sends out information about coming price changes or discounts. This helps me to buy a stock of tires at the old price. It also helps me to plan my advertising campaigns.
Too much boasting.	A new model appears and they boast about it too much. A competitor had the same tread a year ago. I don't think this is right.
This type of research is too rare.	Nowadays, the market situation should be examined constantly. I hope that what you tell them will lead to some improvements.
Lack of help in preparing ads.	National once provided us with master layouts and films for use in magazines. All we had to do was insert our company name, and the ads were ready.
The division of sales into the retail channels is unjust.	As independent retailers, we get a different discount than Råtorp's own retail chain. So from the very beginning, they have better profits, which is unjust.

Negative Incidents	Detailed Comments and Responses to Probing Questions
I don't have any certificate from the company yet.	I've worked with Råtorp from the very beginning, and I don't have any certificate yet. I have one from National.
They don't care . about service quality	Regarding service, they care more about quantity than quality in providing outlets. It seems like anyone can put a sign out and be an authorized dealer.
Frequent price changes.	The prices keep changing all the time, they go up and up every few months.
No correspondence from Råtorp.	I can't remember when I last received anything from Råtorp. I don't feel much of a bond, any interest in how we are doing. In the case of National, we have regular correspondence. I don't know anybody from Råtorp.
Some tires are loud and slippery.	I mean the tires for faster cars. You can lose a customer who prefers foreign tires for better cars.
Too small assortment of tires.	Lack of tires for faster cars—size 16, 17. There is also a lack of special or directed treads.

■ CIT Analysis Worksheet ■	
Benefit Category	Satisfaction Attributes
1.	
2.	
3.	
4.	
5.	
6.	
7.	
8.	
9.	
10.	

■ 3. Reader Exercise for Chapter Six

In this exercise, the object is to practice the steps involved in setting priorities based on the results of a customer satisfaction survey.

Background

Råtorp Tire Company conducted a series of qualitative interviews with several members from Galileo, an independent chain of retailers that sells, installs, and services Råtorp tires for automobiles, vans, and light trucks. These interviews were used to develop a series of satisfaction attributes and benefit categories like the ones produced in Section 2 of this appendix. A satisfaction survey was developed on the basis of these attributes and benefits. The survey asked two hundred Galileo dealers to rate Råtorp Tire Company, National Tire Company, and a group of other companies referred to here as Import Brands on each of the attributes. The dealers also rated the three suppliers on several overall satisfaction and loyalty questions (such as overall satisfaction, overall performance relative to expectations, willingness to recommend the supplier's tires to customers, and likelihood of buying more tires from the supplier).

A statistical analysis determined the impact of each benefit category on satisfaction. The impact scores indicate the degree to which a change in a benefit (such as tire products) increases overall satisfaction and subsequent loyalty. For example, an impact score of 0.30 for tire products means that a 10 percent increase in customer evaluations of tire products increases overall satisfaction by 3 percent. The analysis also provides levels of performance for each of these categories. These performance scores represent weighted averages across the attributes in each benefit category and are reported on a scale from 0 to 100.

Problem

The immediate focus in on the benefit categories, which include (1) tire products, (2) sales material and support, (3) sales department and local sales representative, (4) promotional activities (such as TV and radio ads), (5) shipping and delivery, (6) pricing, (7) complaint handling, and (8) discounts and interest payments.

Your task is to evaluate the output of the analysis and develop strategic priorities for Råtorp with respect to its Galileo customers. Figures A.1, A.2, and A.3 present the performance and impact scores for each of the three suppliers included in the Galileo survey (Råtorp, National, and Import Brands as a group). Råtorp and National are traditional competitors in Råtorp's home market and compete very directly. Each competes more indirectly with Import Brands for their share of distribution. Note that, because promotional activities do not generally apply to the Import Brands as a group, these suppliers are not rated on this benefit.

More specifically, we are asking you to develop a set of explicit strategy recommendations for Råtorp on the basis of the

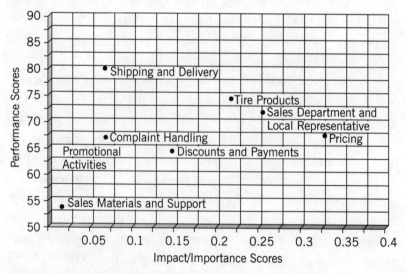

Figure A.1. Råtorp Tire Company Satisfaction Results

satisfaction results, including what areas are the highest priorities for improvement. The last page of the case contains a blank matrix to help summarize your recommendations.

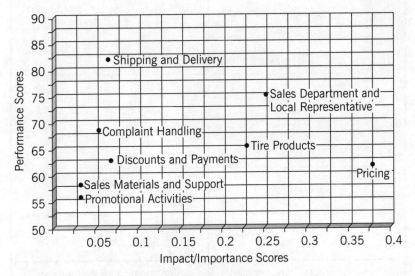

Figure A.2. National Tire Company Satisfaction Results

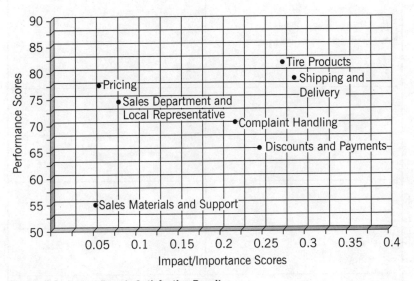

Figure A.3. Import Brands Satisfaction Results

■ Priority-Setting Matrix for Råtorp ■	
Low Impact/High Performance (Maintain or Reduce Investment)	High Impact/High Performance (Competitive Advantage: Maintain!)
1.	1.
2.	2.
3.	3.
4.	4.
5.	5.
6.	6.
Low Impact/Low Performance (Inconsequential)	High Impact/Low Performance (Competitive Vulnerability: Improve!)
1.	1.
2.	2.
3.	3.
4.	4.
5.	5.
6.	6.

Appendix B

NACS Customer Satisfaction Survey

H ere is the full text of the satisfaction survey described in Chapter Four. The sections in normal text or lowercase italics form the interviewer's actual script; those in capital letters are instructions either to the interviewer (plain type) or the coder (italics).

Hello, my name is _____ of [INSERT AFFILIATION] and I am conducting research to determine customers' satisfaction with convenience stores. Could I please speak to the person residing in this household who has had the most recent birthday, between 18 and 84 years of age?

    1   YES, CONTINUE WITH INTERVIEW
    2   NOT AVAILABLE, SCHEDULE CALL BACK
    3   REFUSAL, THANK AND TERMINATE

Thank you for agreeing to speak with me. We are conducting a survey for the National Association of Convenience Stores. We are interested in getting customers' opinions regarding convenience store performance in order to help improve the quality of stores and the service they provide. Your participation in this survey is most appreciated and provides you with an opportunity to contribute to these improvements.

1. Have you shopped at a convenience store in the last three months? Just for clarification, a convenience store is *not* a large chain grocery store, a drug store, a discount store, or a mass merchandiser.

    1   Yes, CONTINUE

    2   No, THANK AND TERMINATE

    [INTERVIEWER: GAS STATIONS ARE ACCEPTED IF THEY ARE PART OF A CONVENIENCE STORE]

1a. Sex [BY OBSERVATION]

    1   MALE

    2   FEMALE

2. At which convenience store do you shop *most* often?

    _____

    [RECORD ONLY ONE STORE]

    [INTERVIEWER: IF THE RESPONDENT EITHER SOUNDS CONFUSED OR SAYS KMART, WAL-MART, TARGET, CALDOR, OR ANY DISCOUNT, GROCERY, OR DRUG STORE, PLEASE GIVE THE FOLLOWING DEFINITION: *A convenience store is a small often franchised market that is open long hours.*

    [INTERVIEWER: IF THE RESPONDENT INSISTS THE STORE (SUCH AS THOSE LISTED ABOVE) IS A CONVENIENCE STORE, THANK AND TERMINATE.]

I would like you to rate [INSERT NAME FROM Q2] on each of the following attributes using a ten-point scale, where a rating of "1" is poor and a rating of "10" is excellent. It is important to stress that there are no right or wrong answers. We just want your honest opinion.

[INTERVIEWER: IF THE RESPONDENT REPLIES "DON'T KNOW" (DK) OR REFUSES TO RESPOND TO THE QUESTION (REF), RECORD AS A 12.]

To begin, I would like you to think about reputation, please rate the . . . *[RANDOMIZE 1.1 THRU 1.2]*

1.1 Overall reputation of the convenience store *chain* to which [INSERT NAME FROM Q2] belongs

[INTERVIEWER: FOR CLARIFICATION, THIS QUESTION REFERS TO THE ENTIRE CHAIN OF PARTICULAR CONVENIENCE STORES, NOT THE INDIVIDUAL STORE]

1–10 RATING _____

12   DK/REF *[DO NOT READ]*

1.2 Reputation of your [INSERT NAME FROM Q2]

[INTERVIEWER: FOR CLARIFICATION, THIS QUESTION REFERS TO THE INDIVIDUAL CONVENIENCE STORE ITSELF]

1–10 RATING _____

12   DK/REF *[DO NOT READ]*

Next, think about the quality of service at [INSERT NAME FROM Q2]. Please rate the . . . *[RANDOMIZE 2.1 THRU 2.4]*

2.1 Accuracy of the checkout

1–10 RATING _____

12   DK/REF *[DO NOT READ]*

2.2 Friendliness of the employees

1–10 RATING _____

12   DK/REF *[DO NOT READ]*

2.3 Attentiveness of the employees

1–10 RATING _____

12   DK/REF *[DO NOT READ]*

2.4 Grooming and appearance of the employees

1–10 RATING _____

12 DK/REF *[DO NOT READ]*

Now think about the product offerings such as packaged foods, beverages, and merchandise at [INSERT NAME FROM Q2]. If you have *no experience* with the attribute, just tell me and we'll go on to the next one. Again, using a ten-point scale, where "1" is poor and "10" is excellent, please rate the . . . *[RANDOMIZE 3.1 THRU 3.5]*

3.1 Stock or availability of products

1–10 RATING _____

11 NO EXPERIENCE WITH THIS ATTRIBUTE *[DO NOT READ]*

12 DK/REF *[DO NOT READ]*

3.2 Brand names of products

1–10 RATING _____

11 NO EXPERIENCE WITH THIS ATTRIBUTE *[DO NOT READ]*

12 DK/REF *[DO NOT READ]*

3.3 Variety and selection of products

1–10 RATING _____

11 NO EXPERIENCE WITH THIS ATTRIBUTE *[DO NOT READ]*

12 DK/REF *[DO NOT READ]*

3.4 Freshness of the coffee

1–10 RATING _____

11 NO EXPERIENCE WITH THIS ATTRIBUTE *[DO NOT READ]*

12 DK/REF *[DO NOT READ]*

3.5   Freshness of the non-coffee products

    1–10   RATING _____

    11   NO EXPERIENCE WITH THIS ATTRIBUTE
        [DO NOT READ]

    12   DK/REF *[DO NOT READ]*

    [INTERVIEWER: THIS REFERS TO ANY OTHER BEVER-
    AGE OR FOOD ITEM IN THE STORE BESIDES COFFEE]

Now I want to ask you some questions about [INSERT NAME
FROM Q2]'s store layout.
Please rate the . . . *[RANDOMIZE 4.1 THRU 4.3]*

4.1   Ability to find what you need quickly

    1–10   RATING _____

    11   NO EXPERIENCE WITH THIS ATTRIBUTE
        [DO NOT READ]

    12   DK/REF *[DO NOT READ]*

4.2   Neatness and orderliness of displays

    1–10   RATING _____

    11   NO EXPERIENCE WITH THIS ATTRIBUTE
        [DO NOT READ]

    12   DK/REF *[DO NOT READ]*

4.3   Positive feeling or sense of fun you get when walking
    through the store

    1–10   RATING _____

    11   NO EXPERIENCE WITH THIS ATTRIBUTE
        [DO NOT READ]

    12   DK/REF *[DO NOT READ]*

[INTERVIEWER NOTE: IF RESPONDENT IS HAVING TROU-
BLE, EXPLAIN THAT THE QUESTION REFERS TO HOW
MUCH THE CUSTOMER INHERENTLY ENJOYS THEIR TRIP
TO THE CONVENIENCE STORE]

Now think about the prices you pay at [INSERT NAME FROM Q2]. Please rate the . . . *[RANDOMIZE 5.1 THRU 5.4]*

5.1   Overall value, for example, the prices paid for quality received

    1–10   RATING _____

    11   NO EXPERIENCE WITH THIS ATTRIBUTE *[DO NOT READ]*

    12   DK/REF *[DO NOT READ]*

5.2   Competitiveness of gasoline prices

    1–10   RATING _____

    11   CONVENIENCE STORE DOES NOT HAVE A GASOLINE STATION *[DO NOT READ]*

    12   NO EXPERIENCE WITH THIS ATTRIBUTE *[DO NOT READ]*

    13   DK/REF *[DO NOT READ]*

5.3   Competitiveness of store prices

    1–10   RATING _____

    11   NO EXPERIENCE WITH THIS ATTRIBUTE *[DO NOT READ]*

    12   DK/REF *[DO NOT READ]*

[IF NECESSARY: COMPARE PRICES WITH OTHER STORES WHERE YOU CAN BUY THE SAME MERCHANDISE]

5.4   Frequency of sale items

    1–10   RATING _____

    11   NO EXPERIENCE WITH THIS ATTRIBUTE *[DO NOT READ]*

    12   DK/REF *[DO NOT READ]*

Now, think about the cleanliness of [INSERT NAME FROM Q2]. Still using a ten-point scale where "1" means poor and "10" means excellent, please rate the . . . *[RANDOMIZE 6.1 THRU 6.3]*

6.1   Overall cleanliness inside the store

   1–10   RATING _____

   11   NO EXPERIENCE WITH THIS ATTRIBUTE
           [DO NOT READ]

   12   DK/REF *[DO NOT READ]*

6.2   Overall cleanliness outside the store

   1–10   RATING _____

   11   NO EXPERIENCE WITH THIS ATTRIBUTE
           [DO NOT READ]

   12   DK/REF *[DO NOT READ]*

6.3   Cleanliness of the rest rooms

   1–10   RATING _____

   11   NO RESTROOM *[DO NOT READ]*

   12   NO EXPERIENCE WITH THIS ATTRIBUTE
           [DO NOT READ]

   13   DK/REF *[DO NOT READ]*

Now I want to ask you some questions dealing with the overall convenience of [INSERT NAME FROM Q2]. Please rate the . . . *[RANDOMIZE 7.1 THRU 7.4]*

7.1   Convenience of the location

   1–10   RATING _____

   11   NO EXPERIENCE WITH THIS ATTRIBUTE
           [DO NOT READ]

   12   DK/REF *[DO NOT READ]*

7.2   Hours of operation

   1–10   RATING _____

   11   NO EXPERIENCE WITH THIS ATTRIBUTE
           [DO NOT READ]

   12   DK/REF *[DO NOT READ]*

7.3 Speed and efficiency of employees

1–10 RATING _____
11 NO EXPERIENCE WITH THIS ATTRIBUTE
[DO NOT READ]
12 DK/REF *[DO NOT READ]*

7.4 Availability of parking

1–10 RATING _____
11 NO EXPERIENCE WITH THIS ATTRIBUTE
[DO NOT READ]
12 DK/REF *[DO NOT READ]*

Now, think about safety. Please rate. . . *[RANDOMIZE 8.1 THRU 8.3]*

8.1 The lighting of the premises, for example, around the store, pump, and parking areas

1–10 RATING _____
11 NO EXPERIENCE WITH THIS ATTRIBUTE
[DO NOT READ]
12 DK/REF *[DO NOT READ]*

8.2 The ability to see what is happening inside the store

1–10 RATING _____
11 NO EXPERIENCE WITH THIS ATTRIBUTE
[DO NOT READ]
12 DK/REF *[DO NOT READ]*

8.3 Your feeling of safety and security

1–10 RATING _____
11 NO EXPERIENCE WITH THIS ATTRIBUTE
[DO NOT READ]
12 DK/REF *[DO NOT READ]*

[IF 5.2 = NO GAS STATION, SKIP 9.1–9.5.]

Think about motorist services offered at [INSERT RESPONSE FROM Q2]. Please rate the . . . *[RANDOMIZE 9.1 THRU 9.5]*

9.1   Accuracy of signs, gauges, and meters at the gas pumps

 1–10   RATING _____

 11   STORE HAS NO GAS STATION *[DO NOT READ]* *[SKIP TO Q10.1]*

 12   NO EXPERIENCE WITH THIS ATTRIBUTE *[DO NOT READ]*

 13   DK/REF *[DO NOT READ]*

9.2   Ability to pay at the pump

 1–10   RATING _____

 11   STORE HAS NO GAS STATION *[DO NOT READ]* *[SKIP TO Q10.1]*

 12   NO EXPERIENCE WITH THIS ATTRIBUTE *[DO NOT READ]*

 13   DK/REF *[DO NOT READ]*

9.3   Availability of car wash

 1–10   RATING _____

 11   STORE HAS NO GAS STATION *[DO NOT READ]* *[SKIP TO Q10.1]*

 12   NO EXPERIENCE WITH THIS ATTRIBUTE *[DO NOT READ]*

 13   DK/REF *[DO NOT READ]*

9.4   Availability of air and water for vehicles

 1–10   RATING _____

 11   NO AIR & WATER FOR VEHICLES

 12   STORE HAS NO GAS STATION *[DO NOT READ]* *[SKIP TO Q10.1]*

 13   NO EXPERIENCE WITH THIS ATTRIBUTE *[DO NOT READ]*

 14   DK/REF *[DO NOT READ]*

9.5 Working operation of equipment such as gas pumps and air

1–10 RATING _____

11 STORE HAS NO GAS STATION *[DO NOT READ]*
[SKIP TO Q10.1]

12 NO EXPERIENCE WITH THIS ATTRIBUTE
[DO NOT READ]

13 DK/REF *[DO NOT READ]*

Now, think about separate take-out food, that is, non-packaged items. [IF NECESSARY: Separate take-out food is things like pizza, hot dogs, sandwiches, nachos, and popcorn.]

Please rate the . . . *[RANDOMIZE 10.1 THRU 10.2]*

10.1 Accuracy of food preparation

1–10 RATING _____

11 STORE DOES NOT HAVE SEPARATE TAKE-OUT
FOOD *[DO NOT READ]*
[SKIP TO Q11.1]

12 NO EXPERIENCE WITH THIS ATTRIBUTE
[DO NOT READ]

13 DK/REF *[DO NOT READ]*

10.2 Quality of take-out food

1–10 RATING _____

11 STORE DOES NOT HAVE SEPARATE TAKE-OUT
FOOD *[DO NOT READ]*
[SKIP TO Q11.1]

12 NO EXPERIENCE WITH THIS ATTRIBUTE
[DO NOT READ]

13 DK/REF *[DO NOT READ]*

Now I would like you to rate [INSERT NAME FROM Q2] on each of the following evaluation statements using different ten-point scales. The meaning of the scales will change from question to question. Remember, when you have *no experience* with the attribute in the question, just tell me and we'll go on to the next one.

11.1 Considering all of your experiences to date with [INSERT NAME FROM Q2], please rate your overall *satisfaction* with [INSERT NAME FROM Q2]. Please indicate your response on a scale from 1 to 10, where "1" is very dissatisfied and "10" is very satisfied.

1–10 RATING _____
12 DK/REF [DO NOT READ]

11.2 Again considering all your experiences to date, please rate the extent to which [INSERT NAME FROM Q2] has *fallen short of* or *exceeded your expectations*. Please indicate your response on a scale from 1 to 10, where "1" means "falls short of my expectations" and "10" means "exceeds my expectations."

1–10 RATING _____
12 DK/REF [DO NOT READ]

11.3 Forget [INSERT NAME FROM Q2] for a moment. Now I want you to imagine an ideal convenience store. How well do you think [INSERT NAME FROM Q2] *compares to that ideal*? Please indicate your response on a scale from 1 to 10, where "1" means the store is "not very close to the ideal" and "10" means the store is "very close to the ideal."

1–10 RATING _____
12 DK/REF [DO NOT READ]

11.4 Now please rate the *likelihood that you will visit* [INSERT NAME FROM Q2] again in the near future. Please use a ten-point scale where "1" means "very unlikely you will visit again" and "10" means "very likely you will visit again."

1–10 RATING _____
12 DK/REF [DO NOT READ]

11.5   Now consider the *likelihood that you will recommend* [IN-SERT NAME FROM Q2] to others. Using a ten-point scale where "1" means "very unlikely to recommend to others" and "10" means "very likely to recommend to others."

    1–10   RATING _____

    12   DK/REF *[DO NOT READ]*

12.   Next, I will read a series of statements that describe different types of convenience store shoppers. While all of these may fit you to some degree, which one statement describes you *best.* [READ RESPONSES WITH SLIGHT PAUSE AFTER EACH RESPONSE]

    [CLARIFICATION IF THE RESPONDENT SAYS NONE DESCRIBE THEM ASK: Is there one that applies to you better than another? Which one would that be?]

    1   I tend to visit a convenience store several times a day for snacks as well as meals.

    2   I am a parent who occasionally goes to a convenience store mainly to buy fill-in items, emergency items, or things for the kids.

    3   I visit a convenience store daily to buy one or two items such as a soda, coffee, cigarettes, or candy.

    4   I go to a convenience store once or twice a week to buy a snack, soda, or coffee.

    5   I shop at a convenience store less than once a week, mainly to buy snacks and party items or items for a trip.

    6   DK/REF *[DO NOT READ]*

Now, I have just a few questions for statistical purposes.

13.   What is your age, please?

    [RECORD NUMBER OF YEARS 18–84] _____

    98   DK *[DO NOT READ]*

    99   REFUSED *[DO NOT READ]*

14. What is the last grade of formal education you completed? [READ CATEGORIES]
    1. LESS THAN HIGH SCHOOL
    2. HIGH SCHOOL GRADUATE
    3. TECHNICAL/VOCATIONAL
    4. SOME COLLEGE/ASSOCIATE'S DEGREE
    5. COLLEGE GRADUATE
    6. POST-GRADUATE
    7. DK/REFUSED [DO NOT READ]

15. Including yourself, how many people are in your family that currently live in your household? _____
    99. DK/REFUSED [DO NOT READ]

16. Do you consider your race as. . . [READ PUNCHES 1–5]
    1. White
    2. Hispanic or Latino
    3. Black/African American
    4. American Indian
    5. Asian or Pacific Islander
    6. OTHER SPECIFY [DO NOT READ]
    7. DK/REFUSED [DO NOT READ]

17. What is your total annual family income? Please stop me when I reach the correct category.
    [READ CATEGORIES]
    1. UNDER $10,000
    2. $10,000 BUT LESS THAN $20,000
    3. $20,000 BUT LESS THAN $30,000
    4. $30,000 BUT LESS THAN $40,000
    5. $40,000 BUT LESS THAN $50,000
    6. $50,000 BUT LESS THAN $60,000
    7. $60,000 BUT LESS THAN $80,000
    8. $80,000 BUT LESS THAN $100,000
    9. $100,000 OR MORE
    10. DK/REFUSED [DO NOT READ]

Thank you for your participation!

Appendix C

Data Analysis in Practice

This appendix presents the discussion of analysis promised in Chapter Five. We begin with an outline of the relative strength of several methods, then provide instructions for using the SPSS statistical package to perform the principal-components regression (PCR) this book recommends.

■ 1. A Comparison of Alternative Data Analysis Methods

Five alternative methods are typically used to analyze customer satisfaction data to obtain performance and importance information: (1) gap analysis, (2) multiple regression, (3) correlations, (4) our variation on principal-components regression or PCR, and (5) partial least squares or PLS. In comparing these methods, we will not discuss gap analysis because of the limitations discussed and illustrated in Chapter Four. After describing multiple regression and correlation analysis, we will use PLS as a benchmark for evaluating the other methods. As noted in Chapter Five, PLS is considered the state-of-the-art method for estimating a quality-satisfaction-loyalty model—but it requires more advanced experience or software (or both) than PCR, which can produce very similar results with more readily available techniques. As in the body of the chapter, we will use the NACS model and data to illustrate the alternative methods.

Multiple Regression and Correlation

Table C.1 shows results from running a multiple regression analysis using the latent satisfaction variable as the dependent variable and all twenty-nine convenience store attribute ratings as independent variables. Table C.1 also contains correlation coefficients from a bi-variate correlation analysis. These are the correlations between the satisfaction latent variable and each of the twenty-nine attribute ratings. The R^2 for the multiple regression analysis (the amount of variance in satisfaction explained) was 0.626, which is reasonably high. This is not surprising as the regression includes all possible attribute variation in the analysis.

The columns in Table C.1, from left to right, represent (1) the question number (indicating benefit category and attribute number), (2) the attribute questions themselves, (3) the multiple regression coefficients (betas), (4) the order of importance based on the regression coefficients, (5) the attribute-satisfaction correlation, and (6) the order of importance based on the correlation analysis. The questions are ordered from top to bottom according to the regression results, from largest (most important) to smallest (least important). For example, the table shows that question 10.1 (accuracy of food preparation) from the latent variable "separate take-out" has the highest impact on satisfaction.

There are two negative regression coefficients. Even though the multi-collinearity was not severe in this case, it presents problems when regressing all the attributes directly against satisfaction. Table C.1 also reveals the problems when using correlation as a proxy for impact. Note that correlations are measures of the strength of a relationship (where the squared correlation

Table C.1. Multiple Regression and Correlation Results by Attribute

Question Number	Question	Multiple Regression Coefficient	Order (Regression)	Correlation	Order (Correlation)
10.1	Accuracy of food preparation	0.068	1	0.515	8
3.1	Stock or availability of products	0.049	2	0.585	2
3.5	Freshness	0.047	3	0.533	7
7.2	Hours of operation	0.044	4	0.595	1
3.3	Variety and selection of products	0.043	5	0.471	15
4.1	Ability to find what you need quickly	0.040	6	0.538	5
2.3	Attentiveness of the employees	0.039	7	0.506	9
5.3	Competitiveness of store prices	0.037	8	0.548	4
2.1	Accuracy of the checkout	0.035	9	0.533	6
4.3	Positive feeling/sense of fun	0.031	10	0.486	13
2.2	Friendliness of the employees	0.031	11	0.456	16
5.4	Frequency of sale items	0.030	12	0.573	3
4.2	Neatness and orderliness of displays	0.029	13	0.444	18
10.2	Quality of takeout food	0.029	14	0.496	11
3.2	Brand names of products	0.026	15	0.283	27
6.2	Overall cleanliness outside the store	0.022	16	0.494	12
2.4	Grooming and appearance	0.021	17	0.332	24
8.2	The ability to see inside the store	0.018	18	0.406	21
9.5	Working operation of equipment	0.013	19	0.370	22
7.4	Availability of parking	0.012	20	0.408	20
7.3	Speed and efficiency of employees	0.011	21	0.471	14
9.1	Accuracy of signs, gauges, and meters	0.011	22	0.346	23
7.1	Convenience of the location	0.008	23	0.324	25
9.2	Ability to pay at the pump	0.006	24	0.165	29
6.1	Overall cleanliness inside the store	0.004	25	0.505	10
9.4	Availability of air and water for vehicles	0.000	26	0.270	28
8.3	Your feeling of safety and security	0.000	27	0.429	19
5.1	Overall value	-0.016	28	0.447	17
8.1	The lighting of the premises	-0.018	29	0.322	26

equals the percentage of variation explained), whereas regression coefficients are directly interpreted as impact scores (the slope of a relationship). The last column, where the order of importance by correlation is reported, reveals significant discrepancies between the two analyses. Using correlation, "hours of operation" is most important while "accuracy of food preparation" is eighth. Also noticeable is the "frequency of sale items," which has a correlation to satisfaction much larger than its impact on satisfaction. These results emphasize that although correlation and regression coefficients are certainly related, correlation can be a weak proxy for impact.

Principal-Components Regression and Partial Least Squares

We now present the results from our PCR and PLS analyses. Figure C.1 contains the benefit-level impact scores from a PCR and a PLS analysis on the NACS data. The PLS analysis resulted in a R^2 of 0.624, which is marginally better than the one PCR produced (0.618). However, the similarity in outputs is clear. The only real difference is that the benefit "convenience" becomes marginally more important in the PLS model. The benefit-level impacts from the PCR and PLS analyses are correlated 0.99, which indicates that they essentially equal.

Figure C.2 shows the attribute-level impacts on satisfaction (the attribute impacts multiplied by their corresponding benefit impacts) for the convenience store data set from the PCR and PLS estimations. The impacts are ordered by size (from the PLS results) and plotted question by question. The correlation between the two sets of impacts is 0.98, again indicating that the results are essentially identical from the two approaches. There seems to be only one question on which the two sets of results show a discrepancy.

In Figure C.3, the benefit impacts from Figure C.1 are plotted against the benefit performance levels for each approach.

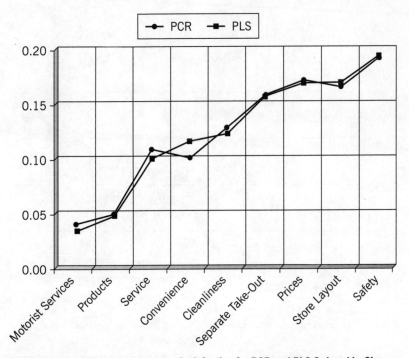

Figure C.1. Benefit-Level Impacts on Satisfaction for PCR and PLS Ordered by Size

The key question to ask when looking at the matrices is, "Would any decision maker come to different conclusions regarding where to set priorities when using PLS as opposed to PCR?" The only noticeable difference is with respect to the position of convenience in the charts, which are otherwise virtually identical.

Comparisons Across the Methods

Using PLS as the benchmark, it is clear just how close the output of the various methods is. Table C.2 shows the correlation among attribute-level impact scores on satisfaction from the different techniques using the convenience store data. The table supports the notion that all techniques produce similar albeit not identical results. All of the correlations are significant and positive. The

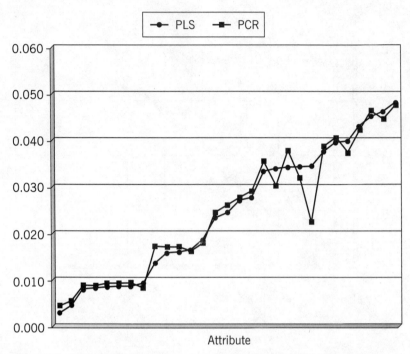

Figure C.2. Attribute-Level Impacts on Satisfaction for PCR and PLS Ordered by Size

fact that the weaker approaches are fairly highly correlated to the PLS and PCR approaches is largely a reflection of the strength of the lens of the customer, questionnaire, and data set used. In performing similar analyses on other data sets, we have found output correlations between the PLS or PCR and other approaches closer to zero and often nonsignificant.

Summary of the Comparisons

PLS is the benchmark analysis in customer satisfaction research. It leverages the lens of the customer to explain as much variation as possible in such key variables as satisfaction and loyalty. At the same time, it turns out that you can achieve virtually identical results using PCR. Moreover, PCR is a more flexible method that is easier to implement given the present state of

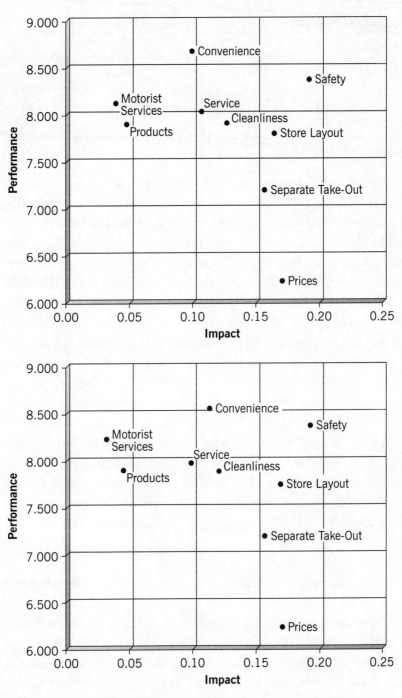

Figure C.3. Impact-Performance Charts for PCR (Top) Versus PLS (Bottom)

Table C.2. Correlation of Attribute-Level Impacts Across Methods

	PLS	PCR	Multiple Regression	Correlation
PLS	1.00	0.98	0.75	0.68
PCR	0.98	1.00	0.70	0.63
Multiple Regression	0.75	0.70	1.00	0.62
Correlation	0.68	0.63	0.62	1.00

software development. Our experience across applications suggests that the differences in the two approaches are inconsequential in those cases where the lens of the customer is well developed, you use the lens to construct a good questionnaire, and you collect high-quality survey data.

Multiple regression analysis and bi-variate correlations do produce somewhat similar results that can suggest roughly where to focus quality improvements. The problem with just using regression to derive impacts is that there is simply too much correlation among the attributes. The correlation is greatest among attributes of the same benefit. This results in impacts that are difficult to interpret. Using correlation as a proxy for impact is also problematic. Correlation with satisfaction is not the same as impact on satisfaction. And the size of a correlation is not always consistent with the size of an impact. Impact reflects the slope of a relationship, or the effect size that managers are more interested in, while correlation reflects the strength of a relationship.

■ **2. Performing Principal-Components Regression Within SPSS**

First you will need to create an SPSS data file. You can do this either by entering the data directly into an SPSS data file (a *.sav file), or by reading data from another format. If you want to use an Excel file, you must do the following:

1. Enter the variable names in row 1 in the matrix.
2. Enter the data in columns, starting in row 2, below the respective variable names. Whether in SPSS or Excel, missing values should be inserted simply as periods (".").
3. *Save the file as an Excel version 4.0 spreadsheet!* (This is an older file format that only saves the current sheet, but can be read directly into SPSS.)
4. Open the file using SPSS. You will want to check the box labeled "read variable names" as it steps you through the procedure.

There are a number of user-friendly options that you can use to explore your data within SPSS. Under the **statistics** option, you can choose the **summary** options, and then the **frequency** or **descriptive** options to get information on missing responses, means, variances, and so on. You will need the standard deviation for each question to be able to calculate the attribute (question) level impact.

The **transform** option is a valuable way to replace missing values. Simply select the variables that you want (as is always the case in SPSS) and the option will create new variables that replace missing values with the variable (series) means or other options. The **graph** options in the program are also easy to learn.

As you work within SPSS, you will be windowing back and forth between the data file (*.sav) and an output file (*.spo). You will want to save both of them for future use.

1. Select the **statistics** option. Under statistics, select the **data reduction** option and under data reduction select the **factor** option.
2. Select the variables that you want to perform the principal-components analysis on. The variables will be the attributes of a particular benefit, or your satisfaction measures, or your loyalty measures, or whatever you specify.

3. Under the **extraction** option, make sure that you have selected the **principal components** and the **number of factors = 1** options. Press Continue.

4. Under the **scores** option, make sure that you check the boxes labeled **save as variable** and **display factor score coefficient matrix.** This will save the principal component (as a standardized variable) as a new variable in your data matrix. The factor score coefficient matrix will provide the weights used to construct the principal component. You will need these later to calculate performance levels for the principal components using the variable means. Run the principal component analysis (click **OK**) and the results will appear in the output window.

5. Construct the rest of the principal components that you will need for your regression models.

6. To run your regressions, select the **statistics** option, and then the **regression** option. For each regression equation you want to run, select your independent variable or variables (such as benefit 1, benefit 2, and so on) and your dependent variable (such as satisfaction), and run the regression. The results will again appear in the output window.

Notes

Chapter One

1. Michael D. Johnson, *Customer Orientation and Market Action* (Upper Saddle River, N.J.: Prentice Hall, 1998).
2. Philip B. Crosby, *Quality Is Free: The Art of Making Quality Certain* (New York: McGraw-Hill, 1979).
3. Lenard Huff, Claes Fornell, and Eugene Anderson, "Quality and Productivity: Contradictory *and* Complementary," *Quality Management Journal* 4 no. 1 (1996): 22–39.
4. For more details see Bo Edvardsson and others, "The Effects of Satisfaction and Loyalty on Profits and Growth: Products versus Services," *Total Quality Management* (forthcoming).
5. Source: Stellan Flodin, Ture Nelson, and Anders Gustafsson, "Improved Customer Satisfaction Is Volvo Priority," in *Customer Retention in the Automotive Industry: Quality, Satisfaction, and Loyalty,* edited by M. D. Johnson and others, 41–65 (Wiesbaden, Germany: Gabler, 1997).
6. Anthony J. Rucci, Steven P. Kirn, and Richard T. Quinn, "The Employee-Customer-Profit Chain at Sears," *Harvard Business Review* 76 (January-February 1998): 82–97.
7. James L. Heskett and others, "Putting the Service Profit Chain to Work," *Harvard Business Review* 72 (March-April 1994): 164–174.

8. John A. Martilla and John C. James, "Importance-Performance Analysis," *Journal of Marketing* 41 (Winter 1977): 77–79.

9. See Johnson, *Customer Orientation and Market Action.*

Chapter Two

1. See W. Edwards Deming, *Management of Statistical Techniques for Quality and Productivity* (New York: New York University, Graduate School of Business, 1981). A. V. Feigenbaum, *Total Quality Control: Fortieth Anniversary Edition* (New York: McGraw-Hill, 1991). Joseph M. Juran and Frank M. Gryna, *Juran's Quality Control Handbook,* 4th ed. (New York: McGraw-Hill, 1988).

2. Alberto Galgano, *Companywide Quality Management* (Portland, Oreg.: Productivity Press, 1994).

3. For a review see Galgano, *Companywide Quality Management.*

4. For details see Robert C. Camp, *Benchmarking* (Milwaukee, Wis.: ASQC Quality Press, 1989).

5. Yoji Akao, *Hoshin Kanri* (Cambridge Mass.: Productivity Press, 1991). See also Bob King, *Hoshin Planning* (Methuen, Mass.: GOAL/QPC, 1989).

6. Stellan Flodin, Ture Nelson, and Anders Gustafsson, "Improved Customer Satisfaction Is Volvo Priority," in *Customer Retention in the Automotive Industry: Quality, Satisfaction, and Loyalty,* edited by M. D. Johnson and others, 41–65 (Wiesbaden, Germany: Gabler, 1997).

7. Anders Gustafsson and others, "Linking Customer Satisfaction to Product Design: A Key to Success for Volvo," *Quality Management Journal* 7, no. 1 (2000): 27–38.

8. Anthony J. Rucci, Steven P. Kirn, and Richard T. Quinn, "The Employee-Customer-Profit Chain at Sears," *Harvard Business Review* 76 (January-February 1998): 82–97.

9. Source: www.fidelity.com, Baseline Company Profile for Sears Roebuck, June 1, 1999.

10. Jeremy Main, *Quality Wars: The Triumphs and Defects of American Business* (New York: Free Press, 1994).

11. Robert S. Kaplan and David P. Norton, "The Balanced Scorecard—Measures That Drive Performance," *Harvard Business Review* 70 (January-February 1992): 71–79.

12. Robert S. Kaplan and David P. Norton, *The Balanced Scorecard: Translating Strategy into Action* (Cambridge, Mass.: Harvard Business School Press, 1996).

13. Thomas O. Jones and W. Earl Sasser Jr., "Why Satisfied Customers Defect," *Harvard Business Review* 73 (November-December 1995): 88–99.

14. Roger J. Best, *Market-Based Management: Strategies for Growing Customer Value and Profitability* (Upper Saddle River, N.J.: Prentice Hall, 1997).

15. Michael D. Johnson, *Customer Orientation and Market Action* (Upper Saddle River, N.J.: Prentice Hall, 1998).

16. Johnson, *Customer Orientation and Market Action.*

17. Claes Fornell and others, "The American Customer Satisfaction Index: Nature, Purpose, and Findings," *Journal of Marketing* 60 (October 1996): 7–18.

18. For a review see Michael D. Johnson, Anders Gustafsson, and Jaesung Cha, *The Evolution and Future of National Customer Satisfaction Indices,* Research Report 98:14 (Karlstad, Sweden: University of Karlstad, 1998).

19. Anders Gustafsson and others, "Linking Customer Satisfaction to Product Design: A Key to Success for Volvo," *Quality Management Journal* 7, no. 1 (2000): 27–38.

20. Masaaki Imai, *Gemba Kaizen: A Commonsense, Low-Cost Approach to Management* (New York: McGraw-Hill, 1997).

21. Bill Capodagli and Lynn Jackson, *The Disney Way: Harnessing the Management Secrets of Disney in Your Company* (New York: McGraw-Hill, 1999).

Chapter Three

1. Michael D. Johnson and James R. Taylor, "Toward a Customer Orientation: A Case of Airline Quality, Satisfaction, and Loyalty," in *Marketing, Strategy, Economics, Operations, and Human Resources: Insights on Service Activities* (Proceedings of the 5th International Research Seminar in Service Management), 799–816, edited by Pierre Eiglier, Eric Langeard, and Valérie Mathieu (Puyricard, France: Institut d'Administration des Entreprises, 1998).

2. Theodore Levitt, "Marketing Myopia," *Harvard Business Review* 28 (July-August 1960): 24–47.

3. Michael D. Johnson and Claes Fornell, "A Framework for Comparing Customer Satisfaction across Individuals and Product Categories," *Journal of Economic Psychology* 12 no. 2 (1991): 267–286.

4. For a review of these methods see chapter 3 of Michael D. Johnson, *Customer Orientation and Market Action,* Upper Saddle River, N.J.: Prentice Hall, 1998.

5. Bob E. Hayes, *Measuring Customer Satisfaction: Survey Design, Use, and Statistical Analysis Methods* (Milwaukee, Wis.: ASQ Quality Press, 1998), p. 17.

6. Masaaki Imai, *Gemba Kaizen: A Commonsense, Low-Cost Approach to Management* (New York: McGraw-Hill, 1997).

7. See Johnson, *Customer Orientation and Market Action,* for a review of Kano's model.

8. Source: Hayes, *Measuring Customer Satisfaction.*

9. Jaesung Cha, senior statistical analyst for the National Quality Research Center, suggested this solution and model specification.

Chapter Four

1. Anthony J. Rucci, Steven P. Kirn, and Richard T. Quinn, "The Employee-Customer-Profit Chain at Sears," *Harvard Business Review* 76 (January-February 1998): 82–97.

2. Anders Gustafsson and others, "Linking Customer Satisfaction to Product Design: A Key to Success for Volvo," *Quality Management Journal* 7, no. 1 (2000): 27–38.

3. Claes Fornell and others, "The American Customer Satisfaction Index: Nature, Purpose, and Findings," *Journal of Marketing* 60 (October 1996): 7–18.

4. For details on sampling and sampling methods see Bob E. Hayes, *Measuring Customer Satisfaction: Survey Design, Use, and Statistical Analysis Methods* (Milwaukee, Wis.: ASQ Quality Press, 1998). See also Thomas C. Kinnear and James R. Taylor, *Marketing Research: An Applied Approach,* 5th ed. (New York: McGraw-Hill, 1996).

5. Michael D. Johnson and James R. Taylor, "Toward a Customer Orientation: A Case of Airline Quality, Satisfaction, and Loyalty," in *Mar-*

keting, Strategy, Economics, Operations, and Human Resources: Insights on Service Activities (Proceedings of the 5th International Research Seminar in Service Management), 799–816, edited by Pierre Eiglier, Eric Langeard, and Valérie Mathieu (Puyricard, France: Institut d'Administration des Entreprises, 1998).

6. Michael J. Ryan, Thomas Buzas, and Venkatram Ramaswamy, "Making Customer Satisfaction Measurement a Power Tool," *Marketing Research* 7 (Summer 1995): 11–16.

7. A. Parasuraman, Leonard L. Berry, and Valarie A. Zeithaml, "Refinement and Reassessment of the SERVQUAL Scale," *Journal of Retailing* 67, no. 4 (1991): 420–450.

8. See, for example, Abbie Griffin and John R. Hauser, "The Voice of the Customer," *Marketing Science* 12, no. 1 (1993): 1–27.

9. James S. Dyer, "Remarks on the Analytic Hierarchy Process," *Management Science* 36 (March 1990): 249–258.

10. See John R. Doyle, Rodney H. Green, and Paul A. Bottomley, "Judging Relative Importance: Direct Rating and Point Allocation Are Not Equivalent," *Organizational Behavior and Human Decision Processes* 70 (April 1997): 65–72.

11. P. Slovic, D. Fleisner, and W. S. Bauman, "Analyzing the Use of Information in Investment Decision Making," *Journal of Business* 45 (1972): 283–330.

12. J. Scott and P. Wright, "Modeling an Organization Buyer's Product Evaluation Strategy," *Journal of Marketing Research* 13 (May 1976): 211–224.

13. Hayes, *Measuring Customer Satisfaction.* See also Michael D. Johnson, *Customer Orientation and Market Action* (Upper Saddle River, N.J.: Prentice Hall, 1998).

14. Donald Dillman, *Mail and Telephone Surveys* (New York: Wiley, 1978).

15. Claes Fornell and others, "The American Customer Satisfaction Index."

Chapter Five

1. See Michael J. Ryan, Robert Rayner, and Andy Morrison, "Diagnosing Customer Loyalty Drivers," *Marketing Research* 11 (September 1999): 11–19.

2. Jan-Benedict E. M. Steenkamp and Hans C. M. van Trijp, "Quality Guidance: A Consumer-Based Approach to Food Quality Improvement Using Partial Least Squares," *European Review of Agricultural Economics* 23 (1996): 195–215. See also Anders Gustafsson and Michael D. Johnson, "Bridging the Quality-Satisfaction Gap," *Quality Management Journal* 4, no. 3 (1997): 27–43.

3. One possibility is the LVPLS program developed by Dr. Jan-Bernd Lohmöller. If you understand the PLS process, this program will help you get good results—but it isn't set up for amateur use. John J. McArdle, Ph.D., of the Department of Psychology at the University of Virginia, is keeping an executable version of this program publicly available (at the late Dr. Lohmöller's request) at ftp://kiptron.psyc.virginia.edu/pub/lvpls.

4. A segment-level analysis is available on request. See Wayne D. Hoyer and Michael D. Johnson, *Quality, Satisfaction, and Loyalty in Convenience Stores: Monitoring the Customer Relationship,* 1999, available at http://hoyer.CRMproject.com/. Working Paper, University of Texas-Austin, Center for Customer Insight, 2000.

5. Joseph F. Hair Jr. and others, *Multivariate Data Analysis with Readings,* 4th ed. (Upper Saddle River, N.J.: Prentice Hall, 1995).

6. Lawrence R. Landerman, "An Empirical Evaluation of the Predictive Mean Matching Method for Imputing Missing Values," *Sociological Methods & Research* 26, no. 1 (1997): 31–34.

7. Principal-components analysis will extract as many components as there are input variables. However, your interest is only in the first component, which explains most of the variation among the variables. That is, it shows what the variables have most in common.

8. Noriaki Kano and others, "Attractive Quality and Must-Be Quality," paper presented at the 12th Annual Meeting of the Japan Society of Quality Control, B1-B21.

9. Thomas O. Jones and W. Earl Sasser Jr., "Why Satisfied Customers Defect," *Harvard Business Review* 73 (November-December 1995): 88–99. See also Seigyoung Auh and Michael D. Johnson, "The Complex Relationship between Customer Satisfaction and Loyalty for Automobiles," in *Customer Retention in the Automotive Industry:*

Quality, Satisfaction, and Loyalty, edited by M. D. Johnson and others, 141–166 (Wiesbaden, Germany: Gabler, 1997).

10. Christopher W. Hart and Michael D. Johnson, "Growing the Trust Relationship," *Marketing Management* 8 (Spring 1999): 9–22.

Chapter Six

1. Anders Gustafsson and Michael D. Johnson, "Bridging the Quality-Satisfaction Gap," *Quality Management Journal* 4, no. 3 (1997): 27–43. See also Anders Gustafsson and others, "Linking Customer Satisfaction to Product Design: A Key to Success for Volvo," *Quality Management Journal* 7, no. 1 (2000): 27–38.

2. Laurette Dubé, Michael D. Johnson, and Leo Mark Renaghan, "Adapting the QFD Approach to Extended Services Transactions," *Production and Operations Management* 8 (Fall, 1999), 301–317.

3. John R. Hauser and Don Clausing, "The House of Quality," *Harvard Business Review* Reprint No. 88307, 1988.

4. S. Mizuno and Y. Akao, *QFD: The Customer-Driven Approach to Quality Planning and Deployment* (Tokyo: Asian Productivity Center, 1994).

The Authors

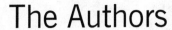

Michael D. Johnson is the D. Maynard Phelps Professor of Business Administration and a professor of marketing at the University of Michigan Business School. He is author of three books and has published extensively on consumer judgment and choice, customer orientation, quality and customer satisfaction, and loyalty management. He earned a doctorate in behavioral science and marketing from The University of Chicago, Graduate School of Business. Michael was instrumental in developing both the Swedish Customer Satisfaction Barometer and the American Customer Satisfaction Index. He may be contacted at the University of Michigan Business School, 701 Tappan Street, Ann Arbor, Michigan 48109-1234 (phone: 734-764-1259; fax: 734-936-0274; e-mail: mdjohn@umich.edu).

Anders Gustafsson is an associate professor of business economics in the Service Research Center at Karlstad University. He is author of four books and has published widely on the interface between customers and quality improvement efforts. He holds a Ph.D. in quality technology and management from Linköping University. Anders may be contacted at the Service

Research Center, Karlstad University, SE-651 88 Karlstad
Sweden (phone: +46-54-7001556; fax: +46-54-836552; e-mail:
Anders.Gustafsson@kau.se).

Index